ROCKSTAR
YOUR JOB INTERVIEW

By:
LONDON PORTER

GO ONLINE @

www.ROCKSTARYOURINTERVIEW.com

To access *training videos* that accompany this book.

www.ROCKSTARYOURINTERVIEW.com

Copyright © 2013 - 73 PUBLISHING - LONDON PORTER

ISBN: ISBN-10: 0983929149
ISBN-13: ISBN-13: 978-0983929147

Cover Designer: Sir Randall Emerson

DISCLAIMER:
The materials and content contained in this website are for general health information only and are not intended to be a substitute for professional medical advice, diagnosis or treatment. Users of this website should not rely exclusively on information provided in this website for their own health needs. All specific medical questions should be presented to your own health care provider.

NEW YORK * LONDON * HONG KONG * SAN FRANCISCO * SYDNEY * RIO DE JANEIRO

DEDICATION

Cali Juliana Porter
London Christ Porter
Our Soldiers who have been in harm's way
Your local Public Library

G.O.D.

CONTENTS ON TABLE

Get *job* help today @
Your Local Public Library

PREFACE

If I were you my first question would be, *"Why should I listen to you?"* Great question.

I've been in the Human Resources industry for more than 10 winters, opened up the Palms Casino Resort in Las Vegas, contracted for Microsoft, recruited for multiple fortune 500 companies, introduced Web MD to the State of Nevada, and have personally conducted thousands of interviews: Medical, Sales, Government Sector, Technology, Gaming, and more.

This is where you say, *"**So what**?"*

I've learned what instantly shuts your interviewer down and what they adore and admire in people. What makes them say, *"No way!"* or *"This is the one."*

Now you say, *"Okay, tell me more."*

I've invested more than $40,000 and 10,000 hours in research, training, and certifications surrounding the art of presenting YOU. I'll share with you my findings, help you fashion or fine tune your interview style, and show you what decision makers want to see, feel, and hear. I'll teach you **how to be a Rockstar.** That is…if you're ready?

And you say, *"I'm ready. When do we start?"*

Right now. Turn the page.

Introduction 2.0

What They Want To See

If somebody asked you right now, *"Tell me about yourself"*, what would you say? Where would you start? How long would you speak? How would you know what they really wanted to know? *Rock Star Your Job Interview* is more than a book. It's a conversation to help you walk out the door, leaving the interviewer saying:

- "We can stop interviewing, she's the one"
- "Incredible, he should teach our people how to interview"
- "Every answer was so concise and spot on"

If this is your goal...read on.

Armed with the information in this book, you'll feel as though you're cheating when you're able to answer any question thrown your way...even the ones you've never heard before. Why? Because you'll understand the practical psychology and simple strategies behind answering the toughest questions ever.

Are interviews stressful? Yes. Are they difficult? No. At least, not if your preparation is superior. Which means you'll have to put in the time, turn off Law and Order, and practice, practice, practice your lines, content, and delivery. How you deliver words is a skill.

Exposure + Frequency = Skill

Speaking of skills, the ones you'll be exposed to in this book have the ability to not only *Rockstar Your Interview* but to enhance your personal relationships and professional circle of influence. Can you say bonus?

If you only take one thing away from our talk, may it be this: Learn more than just how to study answers to questions, develop your personal **framework of power** to answer any question you'll ever be asked. This book will help you cross that finish line.

We're excited because you now have an *advantage over other candidates* who aren't willing to invest in themselves.

What does it feel like when you get **"The Call?"**

Close your eyes and imagine your new employer saying, *"Welcome aboard.*" It's euphoric right? That's why the RYI (*Rockstar Your Interview*) program exists. I live for you to tell our Team you just got The Call.

What's unique about this program?

I'm excited you asked. This book is complimented by an online video program at www.RockStarYourInterview.com, which shows you how to practice these skills. Our staff has invested more than 2,500 hours in this program to help you demonstrate Mental 6pack skills through the vehicle of your answers:

What's a Mental 6Pack? It's a carefully engineered group of six core skills that creates mental abs of steel and the ability to Rockstar any interview.

- Body Language
- Emotional Intelligence
- Mental Toughness
- Mega Memory
- Critical Thinking
- Conflict Resolution

Enough talk. Put your helmet on and let's ride.

EXACTLY WHAT THEY WANT TO SEE

Make no mistake about it the interview is the beginning of an intimate relationship. In the first 90 seconds they'll determine if they like you, can trust you, and if you bring value to the organization. Here are three majors they want to see.

1. Problem Solver (not problem creator)
They want to hear and be shown how you think. Henry Ford, the automaker icon said, *"my best friend is the one who brings out the best in me."* Look at your resume. Identify the times you had challenges and see what positive skills it brought out of you.

2. Relationship Skills
I apologize for having to say what should be obvious. The ability to demonstrate you can build, maintain, and salvage broken relationships is crucial. It's not who you know, it's who you know that will put their reputation on the line for you.

One relationship can be the difference between a $77,000 or $135,000 salary for the same position.

3. A Finisher
Like my grandma said, *"finish what you start baby"*! Interviewers want to see that you consistently follow through and finish: High school, college, your PHD program, sales training, closing the deal, **answering the interview question asked**, finishing your train of thought, zipping your pants, and so on.

1

Forward To Basics

Horrible common errors

You'd be surprised and in some cases shocked if you saw some of the simple mistakes highly educated and intellectual people make on the interview platform. I'll only say this once. Underestimate the basics at your own risk. If you're currently a confident Interview Rockstar brushing up on your interview stage presence, quickly review the basics. Even the best performers necessitate practice. For the rest of us on tour for the first time, take copious notes.

Is that clock working?

You're late? Really? The three rules for being late:

1. Call someone...anyone to notify them.
2. Do not make excuses of any kind.
3. Accept responsibility and keep your apology short.

Example: "Sorry Jane, I misjudged how heavy the morning traffic would be when I test drove the route yesterday, my fault completely."

What this statement says about you:
You were proactive to 'test drive' the route, you miscalculated, you took responsibility, you apologized, and you moved on.

TMI- Too Much Information:
No matter how well the interview is going, how nervous you are, or how self-conscious you become before you're asked the first question, keep your personal information personal.

Guys: Your back-pimples, hemorrhoids, pimp status, shaved legs, bench press max, tequila shot record, and intimate fetishes (yes, a candidate actual went there) are your business not theirs.

Ladies: Your tender waxed area, menstrual cycle, ear wax problem, uncomfortable bra, G-string location issue, sweaty glut crevice, best friend's-mother's-brother's-sister's-nephew's ingrown toe nail issue is not interview conversation. Please don't make me continue.

Is something behind me?
Listen close. Eye contact or lack thereof, can either start the interview on

a good note or begin the first swirl of a flushed toilet.

I had a candidate sit down and stare at the 10 o'clock position just over my right shoulder. His eyes occasionally met mine, but sheepishly. After 3 minutes in I turned around and asked, "What do you see?" He said, "That picture...it's calming." And mind you, this wasn't an art curator interview.

He continued to stare at the "calming picture" until I ended the interview early and reset my strange meter back to zero. It was pegged on ten. You can't make this stuff up.

During the interview, at least 80% of the time should be direct eye contact with the occasional glance away when thinking about or describing an answer. Eyes help convey enthusiasm, honesty, commitment, and other attributes your interviewer wants to *see* as well as hear.

Be like Jesus? Really?

Slow down pilgrim, it's not what you think. Micro-stories are powerful tools when interviewing. Why? Because it indirectly answers the question asked, other questions not asked, and brings the interviewer into your world. And when done well...they're entertaining.

Stories provide evidence you're a personality not a commodity. Let the other candidates regurgitate buzz words and sound like drones as you master the micro-story like Jesus, Native American Elders, and African Shamans. You will stand out among the rest. I guarantee it. Did I just sound like a used car salesmen?

You hated what?

Even when you have a legitimate reason to hate your boss, company, a specific situation, or a combination of the three...take the high road.

When the interviewer hears you speak bad of someone else or a situation, it speaks to at least three major flaws in your candidacy.

1. You do not take accountability for your actions.
2. You handle conflict poorly.
3. You're not an emotionally savvy person.

If you're like I used to be before anger management classes (age 11 and again at 17), get professional help before who you are keeps you from being where you want to be.

Now I feel nasty?
When greeting your interviewer, look her directly in the eye and provide a firm hand shake. Please, no bone crushing or wet noddle handshakes. Remember, interviewers are human too and some of us are borderline anal-alien about hygiene. If an interviewer is apprehensive about what's on her hand after she shakes yours, you're toast. Scientifically speaking, her attention will be divided between what's on her hand and your answers.

Quick Handshake tips:
Ice Man Hands: Rub them together before you shake (like Mr. Miyagi in the Karate Kid Movie).

Clammy Tammy Hands: Wipe the moisture on your pant leg or shirt-side before shaking hands.

Sand Paper Hands: The night prior, scrub your hands with micro beads and use lotion to moisturize them. Repeat in the morning.

Gardener Hands: Please clean any visible dirt under your nails and trim the edges evenly prior to your interview.

The key to a quality handshake: Hold your hand firm and allow the other person to apply the pressure. Match the pressure they use. Sounds easy, right? For those of us who can't walk and chew gum at the same time, it's a learned skill.

(30 second Handshake video training @
www.rockstaryourinterview.com)

Do I Smell Weed?

No, not marijuana. It's just a catchy phrase; however, I did have a candidate have her portfolio dropped off that owned the scent of northern lights hydroponic marijuana. At least, that's what my assistant said it was. How would I know?

Smokers R Us:
This is simple, the more you smell like smoke while interviewing, the less likely your chances will be to earn the position (in most cases). Keep in mind, the interviewer brings into the room, her knowledge of current employees. She's thinking about actual people you'd be in close proximity with, interacting with on a high frequency, and how they'd respond to you: Mary's asthma, Tom's hyper-sensitive skin condition, Henry's smoker's phobia, and Ashley's tobacco allergies. Negative reactions of current employees have a direct impact on morale, productivity, and your chances of earning the position.

Tips for Smokers:
1. Hang the your clothes you'll wear to the interview outside your smoker's home prior to the day your interview.

2. Have your outfit dry cleaned before you interview.

3. Body hair traps and holds heavy scents. Shampoo and condition your hair thoroughly before the interview. ALL body hair.

4. If possible, don't smoke before your interview.

5. Use smoking as a reward for after you Rockstar your interview.

6. For your own health, investigate ways to help you stop smoking today...and this won't be an issue.

"Go ahead, the Surf and Turf's my favorite too."

If you get the most expensive thing on the menu, enjoy that meal because the *"no, thanks"* you'll get later won't taste good.

Interviews over any meal have more road side bombs than U.S. military trails in Afghanistan. Smacking your food, salting your food before tasting it, how you treat the waitress, sauce on your blouse, drinking from someone else's water glass, need I go on?

If you can avoid a food interview, do so. If you can't, keep this next sentence firm in your mind's eye. It's not about the food, it's about sticking the interview like an Olympic gymnast's dismount!

Here's the skinny. The research is wide and deep. In a food setting, your natural behaviors and tendencies stand out front and center. Think about how many meals you've had over your lifetime. 20,000 – 50,000? Do you think your physical body has developed some habits?

So, the idea is to stay focused, clear, concise, and energetic. Feed your body brain-food during an interview. Who cares what you like? Feed your brain power or be obtuse and don't.

Interview Friendly Meals: Grilled chicken salad over spinach/mixed greens, grilled fish/steamed veggies, protein smoothie, or fresh green juices. Let the nutritionist in you come out.

Interview Over Meals: Surf and Turf, large meats, mashed potatoes, spaghetti, heavy sauce dishes, any type of bread. It pains me to tell you no bread because I'm a self-proclaimed bread whore. But, I digress. Next topic.

Perfume:
There is a difference between a scent and a smell. A little goes a long way.

INTERVIEWER: "She's got everything we're looking for, but that smell would drive me crazy."

ME: "That's an easy fix. We can talk to her about it. Outside of her dynamic skills, how will her personality fit with the team?"

INTEVIEWER: "I don't know, I can't get past wanting to throw up. I'm being fatuous, huh?"

ME: "Just a wee bit."

INTERVIEWER: "Maybe...but that smell would drive other people crazy too. It may sound trivial, but I don't need another small issue to add to everything else."

The lesson is:

Wear ¼ the cologne or perfume you usually wear, if any at all. Test how clean and crisp your scent is with at least 3 other people who will be brutality honest with you. When in doubt, don't wear any.

SEX:

I could bore you with an armada of research showing how men are 20% more overconfident than women in many arenas of life. The 'interview' is no exception.

At the end of a phone interview, I had a candidate say, *"I don't want to waste my time. Before I come in, what can you offer me?"*

I offered him good luck and hung up the phone.

Too many bananas can give you potassium poisoning. Confidence is another 'good thing' that can be lethal in high doses. A couple teaspoons of skill along with a pinch of please, thank you, and enthusiasm is all that's needed for interview's sake.

Source: Measuring Usability: By: Jeff Sauro: Are Men Overconfident Users?: June 12, 2012

Don't be tone deaf:

A musician can play their individual beat as long as they follow the tone, pitch, and speed of the rest of the band. So too is true for the interview. When it comes to tone, pitch, and speed, do your best to match the person across the table. Don't mimic them just move in their direction style-wise. If they talk fast and you talk slow, pick up your speed. If they talk loud and you talk soft, raise your tone. You should be in key with each other to make the perfect harmony.

What I'm really asking you to do is:

"Practice being comfortable being uncomfortable"

Interviewers like to hear and see variety. Whatever your natural style of speaking is, stretch yourself and practice delivering outside of your normal tone to add variety.

When you're tempted to lie:
Don't. If you choose to lie about: Where you worked, when, what you did, school, certificates...just accept what comes next. This is the instantaneous digital age. Sooner or later, your hidden truth will bubble up.

I know these points sound trivial and elementary; however, when you really want a position and your stress hormones kick in, sometimes you can't even spell your own name. Therefore, make these items a part of your mental checklist so you can invest your interview energy on the interview.

LEGAL EAGLE EYES
When it comes to discrimination in the workplace and during the interview process, there are corresponding laws you should be aware of. This is the *Readers Digest* version of how the EEOC (Equal Employment Opportunity Commission) acts as an enforcement agency. To learn more, go to the source at: http://www.eeoc.gov.

1. Title VII (7) of the **Civil Rights Act of 1964**: protects against employment discrimination based on race, color, religion, sex, or national origin. NOTE: Same sex discrimination is currently not a protected class.

2. **Age Discrimination in Employment Act of 1967**: or ADEA protects people 40 years of age and older.

3. **Civil Rights Act of 1991**: provides the potential for damages in cases of intentional discrimination in employment.

4. Title I (1) and Title V (5) of the **Americans with Disabilities Act of 1990**: or ADA prohibits employment discrimination against qualified individuals with disabilities in the private sector, state, and local governments.

If you're anxious to get right to the

question and answer section,

skip to chapter 5.

Remember to

return to this page and discover the

power and importance of

'who you are',

inside chapters 2, 3, and 4.

~London

2

Branding You

Discovering your value

Which car gives you goose bumps? What's your favorite spice to cook with? Your favorite color? Was it different when you were ten years old? Which part of your body gets cold first? What two pet peeves set you off instantly?

Let's get one thing straight. You better know who you are before stepping foot into an interview situation. Period.

At Harvard University, I retrieved a book by Napoleon Hill called *The Law of Success*. Lesson one, chapter one, page one, is labeled Definite Purpose. The lesson rolls out the carpet of being certain about what direction in which you purposely steer your career. I respectfully disagree with the beginning of Mr. Hill's book.

You must first have a definite purpose of who you are internally before you can chart a definite career path externally. Recently, CNN Money reported, 41% of college grads "are stuck" in jobs that don't require a degree.
Source: http://money.cnn.com/2013/04/30/pf/college/college-grads-jobs/index.html

If you are a victim personality stop reading now. This book is not for you. Referring back to the article statistics, I believe 41% of recent college grads chose a position. It so happens those particular jobs didn't require degrees. The students had a choice. The lesson is take control of your choices or be controlled by them.

Now that you want to sock me in the face, let's get started. University You is the first higher institution we should attend.

"When you present yourself as a personality not a commodity there is no competition."

Think quickly, what steps can you take to understanding 'who' you are?

How can you harness your individual skill and what value you provide to others?

1. Determine Your Emotional Appeal:

Don't guess how you affect others. Be scientific. Observe and listen to what others say about your personality and how it makes them feel. Do people love being around you because you're wicked creative, because you can catch an error in any document, or because you're always insanely funny and make their day go by faster?

Ask yourself:

- How do I make people feel?
- Who benefits by working with me?
- What common words do people use to describe me?

2. Determine Your Core Theme

At Nike's core is "athletic performance," BMW's is "the ultimate driving machine," and Subway's is "Eat Fresh." It's not necessary to hire an ad agency to develop your core theme. However, ask yourself several questions that guide you to the center of who you are. It could be as simple as "creative," "power listener," or "educator."

Ask yourself:

1. What professional arena am I in? (or want to be in)
2. What adjectives clearly describe my ideal work?
3. What target audience do I want to serve?

3. Determine Your Value

How often does what you know or do solve other people's problems? Please mentally underline that last sentence. Your value is determined by how people perceive you. Are you viewed as a instrument to help them get to the finish line of any race they begin? For example: Your graphic design skills for a website, conflict resolution skills for a merger and acquisition, or your tonality listening skills as a piano teacher.

Ask yourself:

- What questions do people continuously ask me?

- What's easy to me but challenging for others?
- What skills do I have more than 10,000 hours of experience in?

4. Wrap That Burrito

Here's how you put it all together. Review the answers to the questions you asked yourself. Look at which words or phrases fit like hand and glove. Maybe you come up with, "dynamic youth educator," "creative go-to gal," or "rock solid strategic planner."

How does this relate to your interview? Understanding your core theme allows you to:

- Accurately pursue positions parallel with 'who' you are.
- Identify the value of your skills, training, and personality.
- Demonstrate you are a personality not a commodity.
- Ooze confidence and demonstrate Napoleon Hill's definite purpose characteristic.
- Have a strong base to answer the toughest interview questions ever produced.

My hope is that you realize you've just begun to develop your personal Brand. Will it change? Possibly. The point is, this is yours to own...and it's portable. Your personal Brand travels with you. And so too does the confidence and unspoken 'IT' factor it wields.

3

Emergency Interview

Getting your shift together in less than 48 hrs.

If you've ever been surprised by an interview opportunity with little time to prepare, it's easy to become even more stressed, discombobulated, and illogical about what action to take first. Not to mention doubt your skills to prepare in such a limited time frame.

Hey, it's going to be okay. Take a deep breath...another one...let's read on...together. We can do this.

Speed shift the gears in your mind. With little time, we need to focus on the actions that will give us the greatest impact during your interview with minimal effort. Agreed? The list below is a flexible tool, not a rule, of what to do. Adjust it based on your experience and the confidence in your interview skills.

1. Video:
The fastest way to improve your interview is by removing distractions. Grab your smart phone, camera with a video feature, or borrow something to record yourself. Get dressed in interview clothes and answer 4 or 5 questions in this book on video. Observe your self closely and take notes on the distractions you display like:

- Busy hand gestures.
- Constant nervous laugh (even during serious questions or situations).
- Lack of eye contact or too much in a creepy way.
- Bad posture (hunched over, intense body lean, heavy head tilt).
- Gross body language (poor facial expressions, crossed legs, closed arms).
- Speaking too loud or soft.
- Being too monotone – Not expressing enough enthusiasm.
- Too many umm's, ahh's, or repeating the same word often.

You're intelligent. When you see a negative tendency fix it.

2. Research:

Be like the news organization TMZ (Thirty Mile Zone). Get your fingertips on every piece of information you can find: Reports, articles, blog posts, financial indicators/statements, executive biographies, corporate history, market position, trend projections, you get the idea.

Use Google search, Linked In, ask your recruiter, the company's recruiter, call the department posting the position, call the competitor's staff, ask your circle of influence, use Glassdoor.com to name a few. Think. Think. Think. How can you get critical and relevant information to make an impact during your interview?

3. Predict Value:

Review the job description or posting. Reverse engineer the situation. If you were the hiring manager, based on what you researched, what would you be looking for in a candidate? What would be the percentage of skill vs. attitude...70/30, 50/50, 90/10?

Get in the mind of your interviewers.

Again, based on what you learned about the vacant position, what three skills do you possess that would be of tremendous value to the organization, department, and your future boss?

4. Sideline Micro-Stories:

The number one protocol that separates an interview from a conversation is the ability to highlight your answer to a question with a micro-story. An example such as:

Question:
Can you tell me a specific time when you had to solve a problem at work?

Answer:
"Sure Jane, our company had a booth at a high profile job fair with over 3,000 quality candidates. The problem was, no one was visiting our booth. A UFC, mixed martial arts, fighter was three booths down and had a line over 100 people deep. I thought for a minute, grabbed our materials and began talking to people about our company as they stood in line. In three hours, I talked to roughly 200 people in line and scheduled 7 interviews."

Micro = The time it took to read the previous answer, give or take ten seconds.

Analyze this answer from a practical psychology mindset. What does the answer convey that was not specifically said?

- You don't wait for recruits to come to you, you go get them.
- Your mindset sees opportunity in crisis.
- You exhibit the courage to take action on creative ideas.

In the medical-device and pharmaceutical sales industries, answers similar to this are labeled the **S.T.A.R. method**.

S ituation – The problem
T ask – The goal at hand
A ction – What you did
R esult – What happened at the end

The **S**ituation: A job Fair. UFC Fighter hogging the attention.
The **T**ask: To speak with candidates.
The **A**ction: Go to where they're located.
The **R**esult: 7 interviews.

Be hyper aware of several focus points when sharing a micro-story:

- ✓ Be specific with your example.
- ✓ Be concise.
- ✓ The main characters in your story are your actions.
- ✓ Your story must demonstrate a value for your interviewer.
- ✓ Your story must be relevant to the question asked.
- ✓ Your story must have a result.

5. Create a Checklist:
A checklist takes the unnecessary thoughts, stress, and potential errors out of your head and places them on paper. Research shows that a checklist reduces stress and errors, and increases confidence. Flip to the Resources section of this book and review the checklist provided.

6. Rehearse:
I once read the transcripts from an interview with the actor Will Smith, and he said,

"Talent you have naturally. Skill is only developed by hours and hours and hours of beating on your craft."

Similar to professional actors and speakers, you have to rehearse your lines and know your material. And your material is you! Practice. Practice. And practice some more.

7. Power Tips To Remember

- Answer the question that was asked.
- Pick a side. Do not straddle the fence with your answers.
- State your answer with conviction.
- Be concise, *yet thorough.*
- Use numbers and statistics when possible and prudent.

4

T.V. = Their Value

Your work history brilliance

Do you know exactly how to pull out diamonds from the rough of your resume? It's easy to get overwhelmed trying to remember and organize every data point with respect to your work experience...both formal and informal. Remember this simple formula when walking back in time.

- Organization:
- Location:
- Title:
- How Long:
- What you did:
- Major Learning(s):

For Example:

"I volunteered at Opportunity Village in Las Vegas for 3 years. Their mission is about helping people with intellectual disabilities. My role was to identify and coach our clients how to perform simple tasks like document shredding, janitorial skills, and following checklists for their work. It may sound simple, but I really learned how to fine-tune my communication and listening skills, specifically with giving directions. I don't know if you know of someone with an intellectual hurdle but I learned how to really appreciate many of the simple things like tying my shoes quickly, driving, and learning a computer skill in 2 minutes vs. 2 days...things many of us take for granted."

Now, let's dive into this paragraph with specificity. Intuitively, you already know what I'm about to show you. However, we are remembering and strengthening this insight together.

Sentence One:

"I volunteered at Opportunity Village in Las Vegas for 3 years."

How many bullet points in our formula did we address here? Yes, we answered four.

- Organization: Opportunity Village,
- Location: Las Vegas
- Title: Volunteer
- How Long: 3 years

Next Part:

"My role was to identify and coach our clients how to perform simple tasks like document shredding, janitorial skills, and following checklists for their work."

What we describe here is pretty clear right? We start out by saying, *"My role was..."*; thereby, answering what we did.

Last Part

"It may sound simple, but I really learned how to fine-tune my communication and listening skills; specifically, with giving directions."

Major lessons are huge for prospective employers. It gives them insight on what's important to you. Why? Because, as adults, we tend to remember what's important to our belief structure, our core behavior.

Now, if we stopped our answer here, **would you consider this a quality answer?** I'd say it's a touch above good because it addressed all the points to our formula in few words. But it's not a Rockstar answer. So, what's up with the last section? Take a look.

"I don't know if you know of someone with an intellectual hurdle but I learned how to really appreciate many of the simple things like tying my shoes quickly, driving, and learning a computer skill in 2 minutes vs. 2 days...things many of us take for granted."

Use your practical psychology hat. What does this section say about you that you don't directly honor yourself for?

- You're compassionate.
- You're an intuitive listener.
- You evaluate actions in your life from time to time.

There are two major secrets in this last section which make it a Rock Star answer. And when you master these two skills effectively and with proper timing, it will be incredibly difficult not to rate you as the top candidate for the position.

1. Asking rhetorical questions
2. Speaking in pictures

Rhetorical Questions:
When I say, *"I don't know if you know of someone with an intellectual hurdle but I learned..."*

Am I looking for a response from the interviewer? Not a verbal one. But I want their mind to instantaneously browse their mental catalog of life experiences. In fact, you are looking for a response. A mental one.

What do you think the mathematical probability is for:

An interviewer who's 35 years of age that's had at least one interaction with an individual who was intellectually challenged? Without looking too much like the evil nerd scientist I can be, let's agreed that the probability is high?

More than 80% of any given sample population? Why is this important? Because you link the interviewer with an image from their past to your present answer. Put very simply, they have an emotional and visual reason to remember you more than other candidates.

Speaking in Pictures:
A quick aside. When I moved to Dallas, Texas from Yonkers, New York, I had a speech impediment, heavy accent, and piss-poor vocabulary. My grade school speech therapist, Ms. Williams, taught me how to articulate, enunciate, and the power of speaking in pictures. I've been developing and researching these skills religiously ever since.

Look at the picture-words we use in our last section. I'll highlight them for convenience.

"I don't know if you know of someone with an intellectual hurdle but I learned how to really appreciate many of the simple things, like tying your shoes quickly, driving, and learning a computer skill in 2 minutes vs. 2 days...things many of us take for granted."

Why should you care about this technique? How can this tool possibly assist in earning you the job, put additional money on your table, earn you an extra beach vacation, or pay your student loans?

Ask memory experts, from any country in the world, how they practice memory skills and they will unanimously say one phrase. I use pictures. When you drop in strategic pictures, micro-stories, and analogies inside your answers and conversation points, guess who's more likely to be remembered? You!

Of course, speaking in pictures doesn't seal the deal, it's just one of multiple critical components that requires your practice, attention, practice, focus, and practice. Am I getting the practice concept through to you?

Disclaimer:
Please don't be a overzealous and abuse this technique. Sunshine produces vitamin D for the body. Too much causes sunburn. Use all skills in moderation and strategically. Interviewers love variety, on many levels.

Here are three job descriptions from different clients with varied backgrounds. Read their resume blurb and think about how they might convey these two points during an interview.

- Major Lessons Learned
- Major Skills Developed

Marketing Manager – Sky High Marketing, 01/09 – 4/14, Managed marketing disciplines for Specialty Business Group and served as lead member of a cross-functional business team accountable for all business decisions and P&L.

- *Championed marketing programs and general business solutions resulting in increased customer traffic and sales, in a declining Host sales environment.*

- *Implemented company's most successful sales promotion resulting in record customer traffic increase of 13% comp, sales increases of over 15%, and profit increases of nearly 22%.*

- *Improved Host relations, resulting in increased business support, 30% decrease in host advertising media costs, and increased exposure to Host customers.*

- *Spearheaded successful employee sales contests.*

- *Pioneered a breakthrough media strategy improving ROI by nearly 100%.*

- *Employed merchandising and promotional strategies for BJ, which continue to drive record sales volumes.*

Lesson's Learned: How statistics and metrics relate to performance, how to motivate a variety of personalities on the same team, and proactive methods to develop new clients.

Skills Developed: Team Work, Relationship Development, Focus, Organization, Influence, Marketing, Active Listening, and Conflict Resolution.

*Personal Banker - **Bells Jargo** Bank-San Diego, CA, Aug 2021 - Mar 2023*

- *Open/close customer accounts*

- *Process loan applications*

- *Meet sales goals daily*

- *Supervise tellers*

- *Issue safe deposit boxes*

- *Customer service*

- *Teller*

Lesson's Learned: How sales goals affect the P &L (Profit and Loss Statement), how to train for brilliant customer service, and how to cost effectively schedule employees in a fluctuating customer flow environment.

Skills Developed: Manager of Direct Reports, Goal Attainment, Body Language Awareness, Banking Standards, Emotional Intelligence, and Focus.

President/CEO – Flowers2you.com, Minneapolis, MN 2013 - Present

- *Lead operations and strategic direction with full responsibility for bottom line factors, including long range planning, global product management, and software development. Provide fiscal, strategic, and operational leadership to reduce indebtedness and improve operating results.*

    Notable Accomplishments:

- *Led the company in a turnaround effort, which took the company from near bankruptcy and declining sales to profitability (sales growth of 45% or $55M).*

- *Gained Board of Directors approval and executed capital expenditure plans of $10 million per year with an average ROI of 13% per year over 3 years.*

- *Opened new marketing channels and established strategic alliances in Asia and Europe.*

- *Developed, communicated, and educated Product Supply leaders and employees who redesigned and implemented an upgrade product lineup for our number one product line (70% of sales), which achieved improved customer satisfaction.*

- *Led a team of logistics, operational, and purchasing*

employees who delivered 3-6% in continuous improvement cost savings programs for 4 consecutive years.

Lesson's Learned: How to select long term vs. short term suppliers, how global events effect the company's bottom line, and how to streamline costs and boost ROI while maintaining customer service levels.

Skills Developed: Leadership, Complex Problem Solving, Emotional Intelligence, Global Finance, Economic Trending, Mental Toughness, Conflict Resolution, and Negotiation.

After you complete this task, turn your analytical eyes onto your own resume. Do you notice anything different? Are you able to squeeze out more lessons learned?

If you haven't already, get your list together of all the direct and indirect experience you have and lay it out on the proverbial desktop. **Be infinitely brilliant** with extracting every ounce of value you forgot you had. Use the headings below as a memory jogger for skills you possess.

- Job History (Formal and Informal)
- Internships
- Education
- Volunteer Assignments
- Foreign Language Skills
- Military Assignments
- Awards Honors
- Seminar Attendance
- Event Exposures (Specific to the target position)

THINK! THINK! THINK!

5

The Granddaddy Question

So tell me about yourself?

This question comes in at least 31 flavors. However you want to phrase it, one of the first three questions will certainly be:

So, tell me about yourself?

Technically, it's a statement and the question mark is silent. And it's still the number one question that, surprisingly, still makes some of you smudge your lipstick line or fumble the football. Being unprepared for a question you know will be tossed your way will send you back out the door faster than you walked in.

Why is it 'their' favorite? For experienced interviewers, it's the easiest way to size you up while simultaneously making them feel comfortable or in control, or to intelligently observe your body language and verbal congruency. The inexperienced interviewers shoot first with this question because, *"we've always done it this way"* or they may not know how else to begin the interview.

"...people will forget what you said, people will forget what you did, but people will never forget how you made them feel."
~Maya Angelou~

What's paramount is that you see this question as the interview tone setter. When you're prepared, this can be your diamond in the sky moment to display three traits many interviewers are salivating for:

1. Skill Level
2. Enthusiasm
3. Problem Solver

Ready? Let's get busy.

So, tell me about yourself?

Or, the same question phrased in a more structured way:

How does your background, training, and education align with this position?

What they want to see:
Ahh, shucks. They only want you to crunch 5-30 years into less than 90 seconds. Is that all? The key to Rock Starring this question is being succinct, chronological, and content specific with respect to the position description. Every thing coming out of your mouth should be of value to the person on the other side of the table. With the exception of a one-liner that's an interesting fact about you.

When I'm coaching someone we spend quality time crafting this answer from a psychological positioning standpoint. What does that mean? It means strategically placing phrases and words inside the answer which causes the interviewer to think of you long after the interview has ended.

Answer:
"I'm familiar with culture shock and diversity because I grew up in downtown New York and went to high school in Dallas, Texas. Most kids go on senior trips to Europe or Mexico. My older sister, Jenny, worked at Red Cross. That was my senior trip...caring for disaster victims in El Salvador and where I caught the nursing bug. Volunteering was a way to make my own mark instead of following the masses.

The University of Texas is where I earned my chemistry degree and I went to nursing school at University of San Francisco. Frisco was great because the hills and nearby countryside were perfect cycling terrain for relieving the stress from my studies. I'm not a huge baseball fan but seeing all the people in the streets for the World Series parade was a surreal site. I interned at UCLA Reagan Cancer Center and discovered my niche during a rotation in pediatrics.

Working with children didn't seem like work. After UCLA, it took me three tries to get in at MD Anderson - Houston in pediatrics. After my first six months, I realized my greater talents in nursing are in administration and dealing with diverse personalities, trends, and statistics. I've been there 5 years, received a promotion to supervisor and earned my Masters in

Nursing from the University of Houston with coursework in accounting. I believe my unique background and experience make me a strong fit for your Nurse Practitioner position."

What this says about you:
1. You have compassion (Red Cross). You mitigate stress well (cycling).
2. You're a rare hybrid, science and business trained (dual degree).
3. You can tell your life story *briefly.*

Follow up questions: *(Based on this answer)*
1. After you were promoted, what challenges surprised you?
2. The nursing industry can be transient, how do I know you'll be here for the long haul?

Red Flags:
1. Rambling is like putting nails in your interview coffin. Make every word count. Master being informative and brief.
2. Make sure your analysis of a company's open position is accurate. The best way to look incompetent is to provide answers that don't relate to the position you're there for.

PAUSE:

I'm warning you...if you need to take a bathroom break, now's the time. We're about to peel back the layers of the onion and get deep into the core of what our words *really* say about who we are.

Let's look at the answer to our Grandaddy question with a DNA microscope. The reason we're dissecting the practical psychology behind this question is, it's a tone setter. The momentum you generate or fail to generate with your answer will make you a hero or zero in less than 30 seconds.

Are you with me? Great. Buckle up.

Sentence 1

"I'm familiar with culture shock and diversity because I grew up in the downtown New York and went to high school in Dallas, Texas."

What does this sentence say about you? If you're thinking versatile, adaptable, and deals well with change...bingo.

Next section

"Most kids go on senior trips to Europe or to Mexico. My older sister, Jenny, worked at Red Cross. That was my senior trip...caring for disaster victims in El Salvador and where I caught the nursing bug."

Stop and think for a second. What do you see in this section? Correct, it says you're a trailblazer, you have compassion, and you come from a family of compassionate people.

You have the courage to travel to other countries at a young age, and your parent(s) or guardian(s) have enough trust in you to allow you to travel internationally (unless you're a wild child and your discipline choices were either the Red Cross or military school). In this phrase, you also show how you discovered your passion and that you have a passion.

Next sentence

"Volunteering was a way to make my own mark instead of following the masses."

To an employer, a candidate with a purpose is attractive. This one sentence with 14 words conveys you have a 'definite purpose'.

Next piece

"The University of Texas is where I earned my chemistry degree and I went to nursing school at University of San Francisco."

This shows how concise you are with information. If they want to know more they can ask.

Next

"Frisco was great because the hills and nearby countryside were perfect cycling terrain for relieving the stress from my studies."

What do you think about this section? Right, you exercise, you know how to mitigate stress, and you're open about challenges you've faced.

Next Sentence

"I'm not a huge baseball fan but seeing all the people in the streets for the World Series parade was a surreal site."

Why is this sentence dropped in here? Does it seem out of place? Tony Horton, from P90x, talks about muscle confusion. He advocates changing up your style of workouts so your body doesn't become used to a routine. This is also true for this seemingly rogue sentence. We are changing up the style of content in our answer.

This statement about baseball says a lot about you and gives the interviewer a chance to take a mental deep breath and catch up with all the content you've just delivered in a masterful way. It says even though you're not a fan of something, you still find a positive moment to steal away from the situation. Do you believe that's what quality fortune 500 executives are looking for in an employee? You betcha!

Next

"I interned at UCLA Reagan Cancer Center and discovered my niche during a rotation in pediatrics. Working with children didn't seem like work."

Specifically, you expressed identifying one of your passions. Having a passion, purpose, or mission is increasingly more significant to employers.

Next Section

"After UCLA, it took me three tries to get in at MD Anderson - Houston in pediatrics. After my first six months, I realized my greater talents in nursing are in administration and dealing with diverse personalities, trends, and statistics."

This says you're open about your challenges. You're persistent. You're aware of what you're good at. You're specific about your strengths.

Next

"I've been there 5 years, received a promotion to supervisor and earned my Masters in Nursing from the University of Houston with coursework in accounting."

Finally

"I believe my unique background and experience make me a strong fit for your Nurse Practitioner position."

You put a bow on your 'present' description of yourself and pitched the sale of your experience being unique and of value to them.

Whew! I told you we'd get deep. Who knew so much goes into such a small question like, *"Tell me a little bit about yourself"*? Do you see how looking at your answer with a practical psychological mindset can help you refine your answer and Rockstar your next interview?

Again, why did we spend so much time on this question? Because it's the tone setter and typically the first snowball thrown to begin the interview avalanche.

Now that we've jumped the biggest hurdle, let's get into a Q&A rhythm.

Q. What makes you stand out from other candidates applying for this position?

What they want to see:
This is a shoot yourself or shine question. They want to sample your level of confidence and test your level of awareness. How do your skills help make the machine run? Do you know what role you play?

Answer:
"Although I don't know the other candidates, I'll look to your opinion for 'stand out' approval. Jim, number one, I'm a personality, not a commodity. I believe the combination of my persistence, professional agility, research skills, and relationship development savvy are unmatched.

I've been on your staff's electronic doorstep biweekly for the last nine months prior to this interview and followed the company's market trends for more than 2 years. To a trained eye in this industry, the indicators are clear. Your company is approaching a financial upswing.

Not only am I skilled, I'm hungry for this opportunity to demonstrate my value, learn new skills, and help you reach quarterly goals. Hopefully, during our conversation, you'll let me know how my skills can make your job easier and your projects even more successful?"

What this says about you:
1. You're humble (no comparison against other candidates).
2. You come with leadership skills built in (trend analysis, desire, and interpersonal relationship skills).

Follow up questions: *(Based on this answer)*
1. Which indicators make you believe we're in an 'up swing' and why?
2. Tell me about a time when you demonstrated professional agility?

Red Flags:
1. You will look weak with respect to social awareness if you don't know specifically how your skills supersede your peers. Social awareness is a critical factor for leaders at any rung of the career ladder.

2. Make sure your analysis of a company's financial position is accurate. If it's not, you'll have egg on your face.

3 TIPS TO BE STRESS-LESS

1. Use scent.
Cut a small one inch by one inch piece of cloth. Spray a scent that you like (lavender, citrus, eucalyptus) on it and breathe it in while reviewing for the interview in a relaxed environment. Bring that scented swatch to the interview and breathe it in 10 minutes prior. It will trigger your body to remember the relaxed environment.

2. Use research.
Know your audience. What recent company information can you discover and incorporate in your answers: Statistics, press releases, trend data, demographics, and others. Decide ahead of time, how your skills will add value to their company and current situation. Preparation = relaxation.

3. Use Body Language
Understand how your entire body is an interview tool and how to position it so it screams out, *"I'm your candidate"*.

Google "Power Pose,Ted Talk, Amy Cuddy"

Q. Who's your greatest idol and why?

What they want to see:
There is a right or wrong answer. Have positive character traits that you admire in your hero and be willing to demonstrate examples of how you exhibit similar skills. The bonus is the ability to highlight the skills in your idol that run parallel with the position you're applying for:

Leadership, political savvy, diversity, communication, interpersonal relationships, mental toughness, emotional intelligence, etc. Therefore, have several 'heroes' to choose from, depending on the position.

Answer:

"I'd have to say my grandfather is my greatest idol. When I was young, he took care of me and made sure I became fluent in Chinese. When I became older, I learned he was the first Asian American member for the California Highway Patrol, the first Chinese City Council member for the City of Modesto, and owned his own fingerprint shop after retiring.

He'd tell me surprising stories about overcoming career challenges that came with being Chinese. Can you imagine? Things I learned from my grandfather would probably serve me well in this position.

I have so much respect for his wisdom and ability to deal with difficult and sometimes offensive people. Nothing ever seemed to shake him. When he had a goal, he didn't just leap, he made a quantum leap for it. And he was doing all this with just a High School diploma. Yeah, my grandfather's my greatest idol."

What this says about you:
1. You come from a good stock of human being.
2. You're bilingual. A plus in any environment.

Follow up questions: *(Based on this answer)*
1. Tell me how you used one of grandfather's teachings to deal with a recent challenge you have faced?
2. If you had just one word to use, which one would best describe your grandfather?

Red Flag:
1. Shaft, Ron Jeremy, Hitler, Kim Kardashian, and Britney Spears are less than positive examples of role models. Don't laugh to hard, these are real answers. You can't make this stuff up.

2. Not making a decision subtracts from your interview score. Saying something like, *"I have so many…", "It's hard to choose…",* or *"I've never really thought about that…"* is unacceptable.

Wrap it up:

4 Ways to Stub Your Interview Toe

1. Minimal note taking
Taking notes may physically break the rhythm of eye contact, connection, and your ability to listen. Notes are okay; however, write less notes and pay more attention.

2. No stupid questions.
Whoever said there are no stupid questions was probably the first person who asked one. See for your self: *"When does my vacation kick in?" "What are the dating policies here?" "What does your company do?"* C'mon man. Be strategic, talk finance, bottom line, culture, trending, organizational layout, and leave the dumb at home.

3. Leave
Even if you have a magnanimous connection with your audience, leave them wanting more. *"Dan, this has been great. I respect your time and would love to talk more."* (then stand up, shake hands, and un-ass the area).

There is one exception. When they offer you the job, stay as long as you'd like. Heck, get your desk pictures from the car. Just kidding, please don't.

4. No Jokes
Don't be funny, let funny moments happen. Interviewers are notorious for playing along with your 'missed-the-mark' humor only to mark no by your name after you leave. Natural funny moments appear all by themselves.

6

College Grads

Welcome to the JUNGLE

Talent and a brand name diploma can get you in the interview door, but skill and experience are what earn you a job. This should be exciting for those of you from Billy's Back Door Online University. And for the latter from premier institutions, you better bring your A-game to match the logo on your diploma.

If your paper credentials are still warm to the touch from the printing press, how you illustrate your pseudo experience (extracurricular activities) as value to the organization is critical. And the content in this chapter is yours to embrace like a two year old to his binky.

No matter how miniscule the experience, it's time to produce gold miner style; sifting through the rubble to extract a sliver of value: Turning the newspaper route into discipline and endurance, labeling the infant babysitting job as emotional intelligence training and trustworthiness, or demonstrating fast pace and sharp mental math skills as the Burger King drive-through-window operator. Interviewers love to see individuals who can take seemingly unimportant jobs seriously and extricate skillful traits and value out of them.

"Interviewers want to see and feel the perfect answer more than they want to hear it."

When you're less than two years out of college, what exactly do interviewers want to see...in your appearance, on your resume, and in your answers? Here's a few bones to chew on with respect to what interviewers are thinking.

Normal: Is this 'kid' a well-rounded person, mentally stable, and is he trainable?

Background: Is she a fighter or a victim candidate? I wonder what her upbringing was like?

Strategy: I have to know why he's taking this career path and if he's serious or wasting my time.

Consistency: Did anything throw the candidate off during the interview, any red flags?

Professionalism: He better have a strong vocabulary to work here and be quick on his feet with answers.

Tact: She better have a sense of political savvy or she won't last through the first quarter.

Congruency: Does resume = answers, do answers = appearance and body language?

Sense of Humor: Whoever we hire better have a personality. This is a fun atmosphere.

Time for Q and A.

Q. Tell me the concrete skills you learned in school and how that translates into value for me?

What they want to see:
Wow, can we talk first before you kiss me? You'll learn to respect straight forward interviewers like this because, albeit firm and direct, they don't mince words or hand you the answer on a silver platter. You're number one job is to guide your emotions to serve you not hurt you.

They want to see your ability to synthesize 4-6 years of school into three or four key skills desired for the job you're chasing.

Answer:
"Sure, Bob. My school training provided three key points I believe are valuable for this position, the organization, and you directly. The first is advanced Fire science. You can depend on me to know my information with respect to structures, protocols, and best practices, and apply them correctly. Agility: This field and your organization changes rapidly. I process information quickly and make sound decisions based on recent information not old practices.

Mental Toughness: My program was no cakewalk. You're either made for this field or not. I picked several tools to keep calm and follow through on difficult and stressful tasks when everyone else was running for the hills. I'm hopeful you'd agree these skills shorten my learning curve, are necessary skills for this position, and save you hand holding time?"

What this says about you:
1. You can answer the question in the way it was asked (quick, meaningful, and direct).
2. You accurately demonstrated value (hard skill: fire science, soft skill: mental toughness).
3. You demonstrated you know what your strength skills are.

Follow up Questions: *(based on this answer)*
1. Mental toughness, huh? Role play how you'd tell a mom her child burned to death at the scene.
2. Give me a specific example when everyone ran for the hills and you remained calm.
3. What questions would you ask to determine how many fire exits are required for a 7 story building?

Red Flags:
1. Having shaky answers on any of your self-declared strengths.

2. Not having a confident tone when describing your strengths.

Q. What activities are you involved in?

What they want to see:
Save the skydiving, under water bee-bee stacking, and volcano diamond extracting comments for after you earn the position. Trying to be impressive, funny, or creative is a superb way to have your resume used as a coffee coaster instead of being put in the serious contender pile. In your answer, be physically active, align at least one of your activities with your career path and be genuine.

Answer:

"When I'm not studying or researching for projects, I work part time to pay for school, which I consider a financial activity. On Wednesday nights, I play on a rec soccer team to break a sweat, and twice a month I shadow a wine sommelier at an upscale restaurant to learn more about the industry, customer service, and demanding clientele.

Oh, and there's this great spirits blog online: ImInGoodSpiritsForLife.com (fictitious site) that's excellent. It has tips for career strategy, interesting how to videos on management, wine pairing, beer and liquor fermentation, global marketing, and more. I'm sure you're familiar with it?"

What this says about you:
1. You are well rounded (soccer, study, research)
2. You demonstrate industry experience vs. only spouting out buzzwords
3. You have a financial stake in your education
4. You know the power of shadowing/volunteering to build skills (following the sommelier)

Follow up Questions: *(based on this answer)*
1. How'd you come to shadowing a sommelier?
2. What direction do you want to take in this industry?

Red Flag:
1. If you have grades below a 'B', be prepared to explain (not complain) why.
2. Too many extra activities can make you look like you're unable to focus and lack vision.

Similar Questions:
1. What's your favorite past time after punching the clock?
2. Where's the majority of your time spent outside work?

Q. How did you choose your college and major?

What do they want to see:
Your interviewer wants to see solid critical thinking skills. Can you illustrate the logical game plan you used for selecting your college and

major? It's really that easy but you have to be able to deliver in the moment.

Answer:
"Well, I was torn during my junior year in high school. It was either business school or a veterinarian college...I was good in marketing and science. I talked to my dad, my counselor, and did my own research but I was still torn. Then Dr. Nancy, the vet I volunteer with, asked me, 'What activity makes time fly by, making hours seem like minutes?"

And it was working with animals, learning about them, and figuring out what their bodies were trying to tell me. From there, I looked at top ranked vet programs in the southwest because I was in Vegas. I chose UC Davis, because it was in the top 10 vet schools and was close enough to get a Thanksgiving meal but far enough to be independent."

What this says about you:
1. You developed a thorough game plan.
2. You used your resources to get more information and make a decision.
3. You understand the value of volunteering (or you have a Dad who does).

Follow up Questions: *(based on this answer)*
1. How did you get your volunteer position at the vet?
2. What was the most difficult client you ever saw at the vet?
3. What regrets do you have for not selecting business as a major?

Red Flags:
1. When you blame or complain about anyone: Your parents, high school counselor, college professors, financial situation, geographic location, or any other exterior factor.

2. Selecting a college based on your love interest.

"There's no lack of resources only lack of resourcefulness"

Q. What did you learn from your college internships?

What they want to see:

Unless you started a .com, national pizza chain, or regional call center from your dorm room, no organization expects you to be a rainmaker of wisdom and profitability during the interview. So relax. They want to see if you picked up skills that would be useful in their organization. For example:

The Industry	The Skill
Hotel	Customer service
I.T.	Project Management
Retail	Customer Service
Banking	Economic Forecasting
Medical	Emotional Intelligence
Luxury Sales	Super Human Listening

Answer:

"My first intern was with Rick's wedding photography. It was a fast pace, high stress environment. I was surprised how much conflict goes on behind the smiles in most wedding pictures. Rick was very strict and impatient when teaching me.

And I understood why at our first shoot. If you're not laser focused, accurate, and prepared for the impossible, you may miss the moment that costs you a $15,000 fee and your reputation. That's what I learned from Rick, in addition to the fast action Canon line of cameras.

My second intern was at Southwest Luxury Magazine. It was a different experience...a more relaxed environment. I learned how to shoot natural light, architecture, and use the high end Hasselblad camera suite. Behind the camera wasn't stressful at all, it was making the initial sale that was challenging. I learned how to call on clients and sell an 'experience' by phone."

What this says about you:

1. You're not a stranger to stressful situations.
2. You don't complain, you tell the facts and pluck out the learning opportunities.

3. You can answer the question asked of you (don't laugh, many don't).

Follow up Questions: *(based on this answer)*
1. Tell me about a time when you disagreed with Rick and what was the outcome?
2. Which one did you cringe at having to deal with more, Rick's drama weddings or the nasty luxury cold calls?
3. What did your boss say about your results from the cold calls you made?

Red Flags:
1. Even if you interned under Melinda Gates at Microsoft's Foundation, don't try to impress your interviewer. Be enthusiastic stating the facts rather than name dropping. Arrogance is not becoming in an interview setting.

2. If you list your internship as a reference, make sure they know. A negative reference can destroy the credibility of a great interview.

Give me a good reason to not think your bad grades indicate what your performance would be like?

What do they want to see?
Great employers, interviewers, and recruiters typically look at your transcripts when you have less than two years of experience. If you failed or got C's in a couple classes, be prepared to pony-up an answer why. And hopefully, the class isn't aligned with the industry your applying to be in.

The interviewer wants to know you're intelligent, have a good work ethic, and will produce results in the position you're after. It's your job to explain, not complain, why you didn't produce a solid grade. A reasonable answer sounds like this.

Answer:
"The Biology of Nutrition was an elective. I took it to learn the basics about living a healthier lifestyle. And I had three of my degree-based classes the same semester. I got a C in Nutrition because I simply didn't devote enough time required to get an A.

I spent more of my time on special projects in my major classes. No pun intended. I received A's and B's all the while working part time. Even though I received a C, I definitely learned how to live an A+ raw food based lifestyle."

What this says about you:
1. You accept responsibility for your decisions.
2. You are able to weigh priorities effectively.
3. You learn from situations that appear negative.

Follow up Questions: *(based on this answer)*
1. It sounds like you had a time management issue, would you agree?
2. Why do you believe that more time spent on nutrition would have earned you an A?
3. Tell me 2 things you incorporated in your life from the nutrition class.

Red Flags:
1. Not having an answer to a question like this is not an option, nor is a 'deer in the highlights look'. Not even momentarily. It's a clear sign of you not being prepared.

2. Using the word 'kinda' in any section of your answer.

You see, interviewers are real people with biases, concerns, and real decision-making fear. This stems from a variety of backgrounds and lifetime experiences. It's your job, in the interview, to answer the questions they'll never ask:

"I wonder if he's too white to lead our urban division?"

"She has an attractive face and skill set, but will her weight prevent her from dealing with the physical aspects of this job?"

Again, keep in your mind's eye, the goal is to be able to answer any question asked of you, spoken or not. Review this chapter, then think of your own questions, specific to your industry, that you would ask a candidate if you were the professional with 10-20 years experience.

What would you look for? Reverse engineering and visualization (seeing the result in your mind before it reaches your hand) are important skills to learn, master, and teach.

Wrap it up:

Tips for College Grads – Fresh off The Stage

- Be clear and direct about the skills you have and open about what you don't know.
- Admit you have a lot to learn. Use phrases like, "*I believe that...*" or "*From what I've seen...*" or "*The research shows that...*"
- Be confident-humble. Illustrate your top skills and mention lessons learned from your screw-ups.
- Be enthusiastic. I pepper the pages of this book with enthusiasm points because it's the number one game changer when everything else is equal between you and another candidate.
- If you didn't know what you wanted to do until your collegiate senior year, stand tall and say so. Then, sell your qualities that relate to the job.
- Be You. There is no competition if you're a personality vs. a commodity.

7

When You're The Problem

Fired? Quit? Checkered Past?

Understanding the general aspects of emotional intelligence, body language, and mental toughness skills help you prepare for nasty questions. Candidates who haven't developed such skills may get defensive with inquiries that directly challenge their character, skill, and track record.

If you've been fired, remember these two words...So What? Show interviewers what you learned, not what was taken away from you.

"A person who never made a mistake never tried anything new."
Albert Einstein

Law enforcement research and experiments show that your physiology and behavioral patterns will always give away what your mouth attempts to conceal. What does that mean? It means separation is in the preparation. Prepare to intelligently answer cut throat questions with calm under fire. Practice again, and again, and again.

Q. A dependable source told me you got fired. I need the uncut truth. So, what happened?

What they want to see:
I'll say it again, interviewers are human. Many of them have also made terminable mistakes. Give them a reasonable explanation with facts, not emotion, and they will cut you some slack. And in some instances, lean in your favor. However, you must do at least these three things to begin to turn the negative tide toward your shores of success.

1. Accept accountability. Own your mistakes outright.

2. Show the silver lining in the cloud. Say what you learned and demonstrate how not to repeat the same performance.
3. Make solid eye contact and objectively speak about the emotion, don't

relive it.

Answer:

"Chris, you're source is correct. I did get fired. Karen, my previous Director worked herself from the ground up in the company. After she was promoted to Director, I was promoted to her position. The challenge was, Karen still wanted to directly manage her old accounts instead of managing me and my performance.

The clients and my new direct reports often got confused because they were communicating and taking direction from both of us. I brought my concerns to Karen and she agreed to change but didn't. The 'too many chefs in the kitchen' scenario caused a major mistake.

Karen gave a work change order to my staff and I unknowing overrode it because of the client's request. When Karen learned of the change during our meeting she was furious and felt I was being insubordinate and untrustworthy. And I was fired.

Now, to her credit, even though Karen has a short temper, I learned industry strategy techniques, how to mine new clients in similar markets, and she was part of the reason I got promoted. What else would you like to know?"

What This says about you:
1. You were good enough to get promoted.
2. You don't have an issue with bringing your concerns to your supervisor.
3. You appear honest and open about what happened (What else would you like to know?)

Follow up Questions: *(based on this answer)*
1. If Karen realizes her anger got the best of her in the moment and asks you to come back, what would you do?
2. Looking back on it, how would you handle the situation differently?

Red Flags:
1. If your face is wrinkled and your arms are folded when you explain

why you got fired, your body language will not be congruent with an answer similar to the prior one.

2. Complain once during your explanation and see what happens. Then come back and let me know how that tactic worked for you.

Q. I know you were happy at your last company, when did things go south and what did you do to try and turn it around before you left?

What they want to see:
Psychology 101: They're really asking you, is there any chance for what happened at your last company to occur here in the next 1-3 years? Was it you or the situation that turned things sour? Did you get forced out? Did you really get fired and you're lying to my face?

Take as much care with answering why you quit as why you were fired. Quickly describe how 'something' changed that made you make the decision to leave and how you could avoid it next time if necessary.

Answer:
"That's true, Barry...I was happy. The first two years, I had 7 direct reports including two managers. I helped two of my team members get promoted inside the company and lost one manager who moved out of state. You can imagine, I went from working 50 hours a week to 65 a week while all three positions were put on hold. For the first six months, no problem, I picked up the slack and repeatedly asked James, my VP for help.

He said the budget was tight and he'd make something happen by next quarter. A year went by, my team and I were making silly mistakes, I lost 15 pounds because of stress and lack of sleep. The decision to leave came when I found myself being woke up by security at the airport. I was so tired I passed out and missed my flight. That was clear sign for me something had to change. And I choose my health."

What This says about you:
1. You're a trooper and can handle stress and work load during reasonable staff transitions.
2. You work 50 hours per week as a norm.
3. You're a good manager (helped two employees get promoted).

Follow up Questions: *(based on this answer)*
1. What other avenues did you pursue, other than Barry?
2. What did you tell your team after you made your decision?

Red Flags:
1. If your interviewer has the inside track on your situation and you lie about why you left.
2. If you provide a frivolous reason or can't clearly and logically answer the question.

Q. Where does your boss think you are now?

What they want to see:
The last thing I want to hear as an interviewer is how you brilliantly ducked out of the office, used sick leave, it's your lunch break, or you somehow stretched the truth to make it to the interview. When I hear that, and unfortunately it's all too often, you just pegged the top of my BS meter. A simple, "I took half day vacation" will suffice.

Answer:
"I took half day vacation. My boss thinks I'm on my personal time."

What This says about you:
1. You invested vacation time in the interview.
2. You have the appearance of an honest and respectable character.

Follow up Questions: *(based on this answer)*
None

Red Flags:
1. Appearing slick or dishonest.
2. Making a joke of any kind.

Q. I must warn you, you'll be working for Nancy Wheels. She's infamous for being tough on male direct reports. A few have even quit in frustration. What makes you different?

What they want to see:
Whenever I ask a similar question about working in an emotionally taxing environment; you better not only show me but convince me…you have a high emotional intelligence IQ, you can resolve conflict easily, and you have developed positive stress reducing activities. I wouldn't expect you to deliver all of that in your initial answer but I would ask you follow up questions to identify the status of your emotional fortitude.

Answer:
"Thanks for the warning, John. I'm different because what you just said doesn't shake my determination. As I mentioned earlier, I didn't just apply for this position like most people, I carefully selected it.

At my last job, many coworkers asked me how I could work for my boss? Most people found Trish too direct, brash, and insensitive to their opinions. As you know, the cancer research industry can be a fast paced, competitive, and hard-nosed environment with personalities who believe they have God like powers. When Trish would bark out orders and ask me, "What's the status" on projects, I was always prepared with up to the minute details and reports. I didn't take it personal and saw it as her caring about the lives that where at stake more than one person's feelings. Understanding her core motivation was key to not getting emotionally involved in her delivery style.

Ms. Wheels sounds similar to Trish, a brilliant woman with an unconventional delivery style. To me, that makes this job even more appealing because Ms. Wheels could teach me concepts about the industry in 2 years when others may take 5. I included Trish as a reference on my resume. Call her to validate what I've shared with you and don't be surprised if she starts laughing when you use the phrase "awkward delivery style"…it was our inside joke."

What this says about you:

1. You appear to have a backbone and answered an uncomfortable question directly.
2. You understand the psychology of identifying a person's core motivating factor.
3. You've worked with someone similar to Ms. Wheels.

Follow up Questions: *(based on this answer)*
1. Tell me how you handled an instance where you and Trish disagreed on a critical issue?
2. Tell me what tools you've used in the last 6 months to mitigate high levels of stress?

Red Flags:
1. Having little or zero experience working under aggressive personalities.

2. If you have a soft voice or the appearance of a sensitive personality that would get run over by your new boss.

BONUS:

During one of the chapters, you may find yourself saying, *"this question has no relevance to me"*, because you've never worked in sales, had direct reports, had a $5 million budget, or you've never been in the military.

"Some of your most brilliant ideas come from studying industries outside your expertise"

When you review and analyze interview answers from diverse professions, you may discover new methods to standout in your industry.

Q. You have a problem staying with a company more than two years. Why should I take a chance on you?

What they want to see:
The interviewer will have a touch of sympathy if you give him honesty. If you briefly describe your challenges, the lesson, and the action plan to not repeat history; the door is open for trust to grow as you being the candidate of choice.

Answer:
"You're correct. The last six years, I've been trying to make my Economics Degree work in a traditional environment. That was the problem. I'm not a traditional economist. I'm a numbers person with a highly creative and communicative side. The latter skills did not fit with my previous companies.

I'm in front of you because I was frustrated with continuously jumping ship and decided my next job was going to be the right fit. During my job-hunt, I came across ECON-MEDIA SALES and researched the structure of your organization and its clientele.

Your organization appears to have a strong hold on the economic factors and information creation for media outlets, news, and television outfits. I cold called one of your economists on the east coast and he shared with me a day in the life of this position.

It's brilliant how you use economists as subject matter experts to close sales by turning numbers into pictures. That's what I'm good at, and what my previous employers didn't have a need for. You don't know how good it feels to finally find a position that screams....me."

What this says about you:
1. You're straightforward and honest.
2. You're accountable for your actions.
3. You take action and do your research.

Follow up Questions: *(based on this answer)*
1. What was the tipping point that made you frustrated enough to jump ship?

2. Tell me about the process that lead you to the point of cold calling one of our economists?

Red Flags:

1. If you complain, blame, or deflect your personal accountability of being a job hopper.

2. If your reason does not pass the 'smell test' on the BS meter. Be you. Be real.

Q. What does your supervisor tend to criticize most about your performance?

What they want to see:

Whenever you talk about your shortcomings, keep it short. Pun intended. Less is more. And yes, be thorough enough to answer the question. They want to see how you speak about things you've done wrong. Do you beat yourself up, blame it on training, or spin all criticism into a learning moment?

Answer:

"When my supervisor critiques my performance, typically it comes in the form of increasing my industry knowledge and connecting information in a nontraditional way. For example, my boss entrusted me to write a trend analysis report for her executive management meeting. After reviewing it, Pat showed me her markups for improvement.

She demonstrated how I could use a visual trend comparison against a competitor, stating that executives love pictures. And she had a brilliant idea of turning one of my conclusions into an info-graphic because she said the digital marketing department was moving toward visual data campaigns.

Pat assured me my knowledge would grow with experience and that's the proactive thinking she expects. I really didn't see her critique as criticism, I saw it as coaching and mentorship and I'll always welcome meaningful feedback. My presenting and influence skills have become better as a result."

What this says about you:

1. You see the cup half full (Critique, not criticism).
2. Your weakness is typical and correctable with time and exposure.
3. Your work product induces ah-ha moments for your boss.

Red Flags:

1. The worst answer to say is, *"I don't ever get criticized"*. C'mon, really?
2. If you don't accept accountability for what you're being criticized for.

Wrap it up:

1. Fired
When you're asked for the 'uncut' truth: Answer directly, speak objectively about emotions, and provide a key learning. Take time and strategically framework your response.

2. You Quit
Whatever the situation, do not cast blame or complain. Highlight how your quality of life, your health, your character, or your individual situation took precedent over the situation you were in.

3. Curious George(s)
Understand that interviewers are naturally curious. Asking for specifics about why you were fired or left your last job is as temping as picking up the Enquirer at the grocery checkout. It's juicy. Discover in you how to not take it personal. Exhibit favorable body language and deliver in the moment.

4. Be Accountable
It's necessary to say this multiple times. Be accountable for your actions. Here's why. When you admit that you are a part of the problem, then you alone have the power to correct it. Own your personal power or give it away. The choice is yours.

5. Rolling the Dice
If your work history has a pimple on its face due to being terminated, put yourself in the interviewer's shoes. Why should they risk rolling the dice on you? Construct your answer to convey your candidacy as having more value than a risk. Summarize with what you learned to avoid future situations.

8

Coaching
Questions

Cool as a cucumber

The upcoming questions are professional sports related. I'm curious how fast you'll pick up the meaning inside the question and transfer it into an interview tool for your specific industry. The basic premise is: Are you flexible or ridged? Can your style survive in an environment with widely diverse personalities and situations?

"Trust takes years to build, and only seconds to destroy...in between are choices."

Great coaches listen to what you don't say more than the embellished truth that exits your mouth. Ladies, research shows you have a natural advantage over men with respect to effective listening, which explains why you tend to do better than men in the 'moment' of an interview. True, women freak out more than men prior to interviewing; however, perform well on the interview stage because of superior preparation and heightened effective listening.

Source: http://www.livescience.com/18495-interview-anxiety-differences.html

Let's listen in on the wisdom from some of these answers.

Q. What's the difference between motivating professional athletes vs. college athletes and how do you do it?

What they want to see:
The ability to turn around the worst situation or lasso the negative behavior that frequently appears on the 5, 6, or 10 o'clock news is mandatory in high level coaching positions...sports and business alike. Your ability and process toward understanding the core issue is exactly what they want to see.

Answer:
"Let's first agree that what I'm about to say will sound simple, but the

challenge lies in the method. A major difference is...the distance of a player's position to their goal. Professional athletes are at the dance; college athletes are trying to catch a ride to the dance.

You need to speak to a professional athlete's desires of what they want: Starting job, championship, mvp, whereas what motivates most college athletes are the vehicles that can get them to the professional level: Elite game wisdom, performance tips, how to select an agent and maximize their draft money.

Behind every action, there's desire, and before that, there's a thought, and beneath that, usually...there's a fear. Understand that and you have the key to their desire and what motivates that person."

What this says about you:
1. You have a grasp on basic psychology.
2. You understand the challenge in motivation.

Additional questions: *(Based on this answer)*
1. Who was the one player you couldn't reach? And why?
2. You mentioned 'the method', what are the components to your method and exactly how does it work?

Red Flags:

1. Using one tool or technique for a majority of players is an incredibly brilliant way to end the interview quickly.

2. Claiming to have all the answers about the human psyche, over emphasizing your neurology intelligence, or having an outdated method like 'my way or the highway'.

The Corporate Twist:
Q. What's the difference in motivating seasoned professional workers vs. interns or college graduates, and how do you do it?

Q. Explain to me how you deal with and filter constant national criticism?

What they want to see:
Like most questions your answer should be unique. The stereotypical answer of, *"you'll handle it, you've got thick skin, or you're battle tested"* are broken constructs. This question lends itself to the illustration of a challenging micro story you've experienced and how you overcame it.

Answer:
"Anyone who says dealing with constant criticism is easy is lying. Ray Means writes for The Washington Globe. No matter if we won or lost, he slammed me in print for an entire season. I swore if I ever saw him, I'd tear him a new page. And one day, my wife said…why do you give a total stranger all your power?

That's when I decided to change.

I took a course in critical thinking and emotional intelligence, which helped me separate critics' comments from who I am as a person and a coach. I implemented stress release tools like swimming and archery; and my confidence grew when I decided to change because I demonstrated how to keep my power vs. give it away like my wife mentioned. These days, I teach my team how to tackle the challenge of constant criticism as well."

What this says about you:
1. You're honest, you've been challenged, and developed tools to manage the situation.
2. You have the skill and willingness to teach your team how to handle criticism.

Additional questions: *(Based on this answer)*
1. How exactly did the emotion and critical thinking classes help you?
2. Do you have an example of how you taught a player how to deal with criticism?

Red Flags:
1. Lying about criticism not affecting you…ever.

2. Exposing a flaw that you did not overcome or do not have an answer

for.

The Corporate Twist:
Q. How will you deal with directors from other departments constantly being hyper critical with respect to your research, presentations, and best ideas?

Q. I'll be direct with you....everyone loved Coach Carter and his resignation shocked us all. How will you win over people who want to see you fail...especially those internally who applied for this job?

What they want to see:
More than what they want to see, the interviewers want to feel at ease and confident in your power to influence, your approach, and experience in similar situations, if any. They want you, as the interviewing coach, to calm their fears about having a losing team, season, or multi-year slump.

Answer:
"Time and Results. To win anyone over, you have to understand why they do or feel what they do. What exactly did Coach Carter do to make people love and respect him? I'd quickly learn how I could be of service to the dreams and career goals of people who want to see this position fail. Then, I'd observe how we run business from A-Z before making calculated changes, although I have initial ideas.

And after we implement these strategic moves, I'm confident the results will win people over. And you better believe I'll link the career goals of those who want to see me fail, to the success of our team so they'll have skin in the game."

What this says about you:
1. You have a methodical mindset and experience demonstrating influential behavior.
2. You understand that trust doesn't happen over night. It takes time.

Additional questions: *(Based on this answer)*
1. What would you do if, despite your best efforts, one of your best performing assistant coaches continued to be overtly insubordinate?
2. That sounds great if you're winning, what would you do if you were

losing and your 'results' failed to win people over?

Red Flags:
1. Not providing a specific path to success. Using ambiguous phrases such as, *"I'm a people person. I can win anyone over"*, *"I command respect because I give respect"*, or *"I've handled situations like this before, I don't see this being a big issue."*

2. By leading with statements about how you're skills are superior to that of Coach Carter's or his methods were in anyway defunct.

The Corporate Twist:
Q. I'll be straight with you, everyone loved the former director and her resignation shocked us all. How will you win the trust of your sales team, especially those who applied for this position?

"You can teach a skill...you can't teach an attitude."

BONUS:

A close friend was applying for the Metropolitan Police Department in Las Vegas. He asked for my help to prepare. Not only did I help, I applied with him to test my Rockstar interview skills and I thought it'd be priceless to see the process from the inside. During the oral board, I'll never forget the question one of the detectives asked me:

Q: *"Do you have a problem taking the life of another human being?"*

A: *"If the life of my partner or a member of the public was in danger, no."*

Based on their stone expressions and the 15 seconds of silence that seemed like 15 minutes, I was sure my answer was burnt toast. But it was my honest answer.

When I declined the offer to join the force, the detective told me that my response was the perfect answer. Sometimes you have no clue if your answer is a hero or zero; however, you always have the option to:

BELIEVE IN **YOU**

Practice, Practice, Practice your interview skills.

Q. Describe a specific situation when you realized you needed to improve your communication skills.

What they want to see:
Think about adding value to the organization. Thumb through your mental rolodex and retrieve an example when your communication skills had to improve because you were in a new position, environment, or at a new level of the organization. That's the basis for what the interviewer wants to see. A point in time where you had a humble growth moment.

Answer:
"My first head coach position, I didn't realize how much I was shielded from the business side: Team Investors, player agents, and a multitude of contracts. During executive meetings, I found myself getting lost in the conversations because I didn't understand acronyms like CFROI (Cash Flow Return on Investment) or EBITDA (Earnings Before Interest, Taxes, Depreciation, Amortization).

For 3 months, twice per week, I visited with our CFO or Senior Accountant until I got up to speed on the financial language and the cash flow components of our business internally and the industry at large. Increasing my financial communication helped me become a better coach.

I now understand our salary cap structure A to Z, I'm able to give players advice on how to deal with their agents, and my negotiation skills with respect to recruiting key players and assistant coaches are...let's say, much better."

What this says about you:
1. You take action on and are not afraid of learning new professional skills (3 months of mentorship).
2. You understand how and where to implement new skills outside of the situation you originally intended to use them. (advising players)

Additional questions: *(Based on this answer)*
1. Where did you get the idea meet with the CFO and Senior Accountant?
2. Why did it take you three months to pick up simple financial language?

PAUSE: Reread "Additional question" #2. Did the style of that question nuisance you at all?

This is the type of question a 'stress interview' would have. A solid answer would be that you learned the simple language quickly and expanded your knowledge by understanding the entire organization and industry concepts. Be prepared to back up your answer with content and micro examples.

It's difficult not to take pointed questions about your ability and results personal if you're not prepared. This is a reminder that stress interviews are uncommon for most industries; however, a stress interview question dropped in the middle of a typical interview is very common.

Red Flags:

1. If you offer court appointed communication classes like domestic violence, anger management (as a result of assault), or any form of behavioral counseling during an interview...please stop. Yes, I'm speaking from experience listening to candidates talk their way out of contention for a position.

2. Let's say, in the above example, if it took the person 12 months vs. 3 months to learn the new financial skills...would the example be as powerful or would the interviewer think the candidate is a slow learner?

The Corporate Twist:

Q. Describe a specific situation when your communication style wasn't effective in motivating your sales team? What did you do?

Q. How do you coach an assistant coach on how to build trust?

What they want to see:

Duplication. An experienced interviewer will challenge you with a question like this to see if you can grow a direct report's skills to deliver the same results as you. The main concern is for organizational success

and positive momentum to continue if you get hit by a bus or a promotion. Do you have the ability to duplicate yourself in others?
Answer:

"I typically don't hire coaches who don't have some natural talent or learned skill to build trust. However, if I did inherit such an assistant...again, I'd observe, ask, identify, and role-play. What I'd observe is how they communicate with players, other coaches, and watch their actions. If I saw something precarious, I'd ask why they did what they did...to understand their intent. Usually, by then it's easy to identify the missing link in their communication style.

And just like we watch games on film, I'd privately role-play sessions with him on how to build trust through words and actions. It's more effective when you show someone their actions vs. tell them. And if this process sounds time consuming to you, it is. And now you know why I prefer to hire coaches who already have trust-building skills."

What this says about you:
1. You're experienced at coaching behavior to the degree that you recruit with specific behavioral attributes in mind.
2. It sounds like it's not your first rodeo with inherited skill sets.

Additional questions: *(Based on this answer)*
1. What would you do if you inherited a coach without this skill, a bad attitude, and it was the owner's nephew?
2. What would you do if your most talented assistant coach couldn't grasp building this skill even though he was trying?

Red Flags:
1. If your answer sounds like you're unfamiliar with this type of situation.
2. If your process doesn't clearly convey a logical way to coach-up trust.

The Corporate Twist:
Q. What's the specific process you use to identify and coach up a direct report to take your place?

Wrap it up

1. T.V.

Their Value – Yet another reminder to always think about how your skills and answers demonstrate value to the person your interviewing with, the position, or the organization.

2. Be Coachable

Great coaches become great because they're coachable. When demonstrating your mastery in a subject, shine the light on how and where you learned the skill. This validates you being coachable.

3. Be Smart

Any modern brain researcher will tell you that thoughts are electric, a form of energy, and cause hormones to release in the blood stream that dictate actions. Use simple tools to corral your thoughts and induce superior actions.

4. Be Adaptable

Have at least 3 micro-stories that demonstrate the skills necessary for the position. I.E. Leadership, diversity, conflict resolution, customer service, and so on. Composing multiple micro-story examples enables you to adapt to distinctive organizations and styles of interviewers.

9

The Library...
Really?

Porn next door questions

When you're reviewing this chapter, look deeper into the questions. Yes, the answers are library specific; however, can you transfer the learning into your environment or field of expertise? Of course you can. For example, how you handle an upset customer has a similar solution blueprint whether the situation occurs at a library, a bank, or the grocery store...right? John Lubbuck, an English banker said,

"What we see depends mainly on what we look for."

Open your mind, see transferable skills, and discover resources to help you Rockstar your interview.

Let's ride.

Q. A patron approaches you and She's furious the man next to her is viewing pornography. She demands that you make him stop. What would you do?

What they want to see:
Are you a 'policy thumper'? Do you fold like a cheap lawn chair when customers get upset? Are you kind, even to rude and obnoxious clientele? Interviewers want to see patience and sound judgment skills.

Answer:
"I'd first thank the woman for bringing it to my attention, listen...and make sure I understood her main concern. In a calm tone, I'd ask what did she see? If it were child pornography, I would verify it myself, trespass the patron immediately, and notify the authorities if that was the policy.

If it was adult porn, I'd emphasize to the woman that the library stands by 1st Amendments rights and doesn't sensor materials, based on the policies I reviewed from your website.

I'd provide a few quick examples like the 50 Shades of Grey book, professional nude photography collections, and the adult magazines we carry. And let her know that if we pulled all material with offensive words

or images, based on one person's opinion, we'd have a significantly smaller collection.

I'd then offer her an immediate solution to move her to a new location in the computer lab. Finally, if I was not able to deescalate the situation or solve the problem myself, I'd get help from my supervisor, brief him on the situation away from the woman and watch how he handled the situation to learn."

What this says about you:
1. This isn't your first 'angry customer' rodeo. You have effective conflict resolution experience.
2. You did your research (citing the policies from online).
3. You're not afraid to ask for help.

Follow up Questions: *(based on this answer)*
1. What would you do if the woman began yelling?
2. What would you do if the man viewing the pornography attempted to show the furious woman what he was watching?

Red Flags:
1. Not understanding what to do when a situation is bigger than your experience.
2. Escalating the situation by taking the complaint or the woman's aggression personally.

BONUS:

When researching a company's website you're interviewing with, incorporate similar language patterns, policies, and strategies that are displayed on their site. The similar 'speak' will make you stand out from other external candidates.

Q. A young child is habitually left unattended in the branch. When you speak to the parents about this, they become curt and argumentative. How would you handle this situation?

What they want to see:
I hope you're wearing deodorant because questions like this make you sweat. But really, if I asked you this question I want to see how you'd keep our customer in compliance without running them out the building.

Answer:
"If the parents began to argue, I'd listen to their objection completely without interrupting and remind myself to not take their aggression personally. In a calm voice, I'd ask them a question to get us all on common ground. I'd ask if we could agree that the safety of their child was most important in this situation?

I'd state the facts...their child has been observed on 5 separate occasions being unattended for more than 15 minutes each occasion, or however many it was. Then make them aware that although the library is a safe place, it's still a public space. I'd listen to their response and if further influence was needed, I'd remind them they agreed to not leave their child unattended when they signed for their library card.

If the couple remained combative, I'd get help from my supervisor, brief her on the situation away from the couple, and watch how she handled the situation to learn."

What this says about you:
1. You demonstrate emotional intelligence skills (not taking it personal).
2. You speak with facts vs. emotion during emotional conversations.
3. You know how to work towards common ground and solutions.

Follow up Questions: *(based on this answer)*
1. What would you have done if one or more persons began using foul language with you?
2. What would you say if they said, *"it's your job and our taxes pay your salary?"*

Red Flags:
1. Making a negative comment about the couples' parenting style or lack thereof.
2. Calling your manager immediately without initially trying to handle the situation.

Q. Let's say you overheard a coworker give a patron the wrong information, what would you do?

What they want to see:
This is a perfect question to get shot in your 'team-player big toe'. Tact is a learned skill and you must demonstrate it in your response. It's important to use the tact that is natural for your personality. Some use humor, discreetness, matter of fact-ness, etc. Understand what's natural and what works for you.

Answer:
"Well Gary, that depends. Let's say it's something small...such as telling a guest they can check out up to 15 items and the max is 14. I wouldn't say anything until the patron left. I want patrons to have trust in us and wouldn't want my coworker to become embarrassed. However, I would ensure my coworker learns what the correct maximum number is.

If it were something more significant, like telling a guest we can place their items on hold for 48 hours when the answer is 24, I would definitely speak up. Depending on how fast the transaction was occurring, I'd either write the correct answer on a small piece of paper and discretely give it to my coworker or interrupt and ask for my co-workers assistance for a brief moment...away from the customer and give him the right info.

Afterward, I'd ask my co-worker if he'd like us to bring this instance to our supervisor's attention so she could cover it the next staff meeting in case others had incorrect information too."

What this says about you:
1. You respect your coworkers' reputation with clientele and feelings (team player).
2. You demonstrate good judgment (small vs. big issue).

Follow up Questions: *(based on this answer)*

1. What would you do if your coworker didn't want to let your supervisor know about the situation?
2. What would you do if your coworker became angry at you for interrupting?

Red Flags:
1. If you interrupt with little tact and zero concern for your co-worker's feelings and her client reputation.
2. If you let the guest leave with the wrong information on a critical issue.

Q. What do you feel are the greatest challenges facing our industry in the future?

What they want to see:
When asking about future trends, the interviewer is testing your Visionary-Prada and gauging how you spend *your discretionary energy* and time. Are you just a worker or a thinker as well?

Answer:
"Without straddling the fence, this answer depends on several factors. The type of library, geographic location, and funding source to name a few. Taking a helicopter view, my top three are Technology, Communicating Value, and Relevancy. This is a meaty question and I'll be as brief as I can.

Just recently, eBooks sold more units nationally than print books...for the first time ever. The data storage, delivery to users, and ease or the lack thereof with various e-readers is an ongoing challenge. Every six months, new e-reader editions surface and the challenges magnify.

When's the last time you read about a library closing, cutting back hours, operating with 25% of their usual collection's budget, or experiencing layoffs? This is more than a money issue, it's about communicating value to the tax payers or the hearts of those behind the funding source. And it's our responsibility to show people what's in it for them...specifically, how our resources and knowledge can help solve problems in their lives.

And solving problems dovetails into relevancy. For example, what's relevant in your life right now? For many people, it's not their local library. How do we change that? Social media alone is not the answer. It's a piece of the pie but only a slice. I have a couple of ideas how to create a movement and renew passion in our industry. But like I said, I'll keep this short and honor your time. Technology, Communicating Value, and Relevancy...are my top three."

What this says about you:
1. You spend time studying your craft outside of work.
2. You're exhibiting leadership traits, vision, and leave the interviewer thinking about your *rhetorical questions*.

Follow up Questions: *(based on this answer)*
1. Which one had the biggest effect on your previous position and why?
2. Tell us more about some of those ideas you have about igniting new passion in our industry?

Red Flags:
1. Being arrogant and acting like you have all the answers.
2. Providing a poor or incorrect answer about your industry's future.

BONUS:

Be on the cutting edge of trends, innovation, and technological advancements in your industry. Of course, you don't have to be the genesis, simply be aware and able to speak on trends strategically and conversationally. Join think tanks or discussion groups on LinkedIn and follow C-Suite executives from competitors in complementary markets.

Q. What databases do you use most often to serve your clientele?

What they want to see:
When you get a chance to show an interviewer how you solve people's problems, *carpe diem*. Seize that moment like it's your last breath. Personalize your answer with a micro-story and relive the moment of helping a client.

Answer:
"When I was at the Harlem Library, we had a large blue collar and 'at risk' patronage. Kids would come in needing homework help and I'd turn them on to Brainfuse. As you know, they can get online tutor assistance in science, math, history, and more....With Brainfuse, I could help more than one child at the same time.

On the adult side, we had a large population of mechanics come in to use Chilton to get diagrams of older cars they were fixing. Mr. James called at 9:30 am every Monday morning with his list. He owned a small body shop.

When I was at the University of Arizona library, it was mostly students, faculty, and businesses as patrons. I'd predominately use opposing view points for school or research projects and reference USA for small businesses and media searching for phone numbers, names, titles, salaries, and such.

But the most important factor about databases is that we can use them as selling points...what we have can solve people's problems."

What this says about you:
1. You have extensive experience working with databases and helping people.
2. You understand the value behind the tools you use at work.

Follow up Questions: *(based on this answer)*
1. How would you help the same individuals if the computers went down

and you couldn't access the electronic databases?
2. Why is it important to solve people's problems?

Red Flags:
1. Being too short or not specific with your answers.
2. If you incorrectly identify websites or search engines as library databases.

Wrap it up:

Library Hidden Secrets

1. Netflix

At least once a week I get surprised by people in my community who don't know they can borrow movies, cds, download e-books, borrow electronic devices, or get free wi-fi at our public libraries. Call your local library today and ask what new services are available.

2. Problem Solvers

Libraries have access to databases like Reference USA to get content rich intelligence and recon on the company and or people you're interviewing with. Get your 007 on at the library.

3. Starbucks

If your local coffee shop is full, meet friends and colleagues at the library. Use meeting rooms to prepare for an interview (White board typically included).

4. Variety

Visit your library today to change up your daily routine, get away from home, or to be in a quiet open space that fosters creative ideas.

5. Match.com

A library can be a great place to get lucky and meet someone new.

10

Illegal Eagle Questions

Emotional Intelligence in your answers

When you're asked an illegal question. *You have a choice.* Of course, interviewers aren't supposed to ask you questions about: Your weight, being married, favorite wine, religion, political views, your children, and more.

The reality is, sometimes **they do**. Whether intentionally or out of ignorance. Interviewers are real people, with real life issues, and are prone to make mistakes. Interviewers have a varied sense of humor, may be in the mist of having a bad day, or have an internal candidate in mind and not take your interview seriously. Whatever the reason,

"Why they ask bonehead questions is none of your business. How you respond, is your business."

How you handle their mistakes is a predictor of how you'll handle an external or internal customer's mistakes as well. For example, I'm Black, and if I can't effectively handle an interviewer addressing me as 'boy' without losing my emotions and administering a rear naked choke, how could I reasonably expect to handle a premier business client who may accidentally address me the same way?

This is where your Mental Sixpack skills come into play: Body Language, Emotional Intelligence, Mental Toughness, Mega Memory, Critical Thinking, and Conflict Resolution.

Interviews are a two-way street. They are interviewing you and you, my RYI friend, are interviewing them. Let's get dirty.

Q. How do you feel about homosexuals in business? On your team?

Answer:
"If you're really asking me am I homophobic, no. I currently have a direct report who is openly gay. In fact, I asked him one day, "John, how do you

consistently produce more customer models than anyone else on the team?"

He said, "I have an unfair advantage. When you're spending time with your kids, I'm researching, studying, and drafting proposals...constantly."

What this says about you:
1. You answer difficult questions directly.
2. You demonstrate experience in addition to speaking it.

Similar Ignorant Questions:
1. What's your take on illegal Mexicans and American jobs?
2. What's your opinion on this gun control issue?
3. Do you have an affinity one-way or the other for affirmative action programs?

Q. I understand you're a single mom with a special needs child. What time do you have to be home because we often stay past 7pm?

Answer:
"Nancy, thanks for being understanding. I wouldn't have applied for this position if I wasn't able to put in the late nights. I have no set time to be home. Amy, my full time caretaker of three years, is wonderful and understands the demands of my career. Late nights, weekends, and out of town trips are all part of the deal. What types of projects keep your team burning the midnight oil?"

NOTE: If you're not able to work a position because of a set personal schedule, say so up front. The job's time commitment either fits or it doesn't. Be honest with your personal situation.

What this says about you:
1. You think before you take action (late nights, travel).
2. You have child care stability (Amy + 3 years = reliability.)

Similar Ignorant Questions:
1. Who watches the kids when you're at work?
2. Which private school do the kids attend?
3. Does your nanny drive the kids to their extra curricular activities?

Logic vs. Emotion

1. Answering a question with silence and a smile gives the interviewer a moment to realize he may have asked an inappropriate question.

2. Give the answer seeker the benefit of the doubt, she may have asked an out of bounds question out of general concern or ignorance.

3. You always have a choice. Decide today what your limits are for ending an interview early, not accepting an offer, or reporting a situation to authorities.

Q. Are you Republican or Democrat?

Answer: Indirect
"I vote on issues, not party lines."

Be prepared to have a direct answer as a follow up. Real estate taxes, health care, income tax bracket effects, and so on.

Answer: Direct
"Independent" (or another affiliation)

"Go where you're appreciated, not where you're tolerated"

Q. Are you married...to a Man?

Even though gay marriage is less of an issue than it was even 5 years ago, research top companies that are GLBT friendly in your industry. After all, your goal when you get hired is to thrive, not just survive, right?

Answer: Indirect
*"I have a partner and a solid relationship.
(or with humorous tone depending on the situation)
I have a partner and an every day dysfunctional relationship."*

Answer: Direct
"Yes" or "No"

Similar Ignorant Questions:
1. It's not a big issue here, but are you gay?
2. Is your marriage recognized by the state?
3. Do you have a partner or a spouse?

Q. Are you Black or African American?

Answer: Indirect
"I'm Barry" (flash a smile or grin for a more dramatic effect)

Answer: Direct
"Black, African-American"

Did you lose a house in the market like I did?

Ahh, the 'I'm on your side' tactic or misery loves company approach. Many times a sly question like this is neatly placed in small talk pre or post interview to mine for dirt when your shields are down.

Answer:
"I believe everybody knows somebody who's lost their shirt in this market. Speaking of markets, what made the company's third quarter excel like it did."

Q. On a scale of 1-10, how sensitive are you about your weight?

Answer:
"One. And you better take a picture because I've lost 25 pounds in two months and I'm committed to my goal of 65 more. I hope my focus on health and appearance won't prevent you from considering me for this position?"

What this says about you:
1. You're not emotionally attached to your weight.
2. You are currently taking action to be healthy.
3. You handle injudicious questions with grace and style.

Q. Your last name is Goldberg, are you Jewish?

Answer: Indirect
"No, I'm Jamie."

Answer: Direct
"Yes" or "No"

Q. I want to be honest, the next 24 months will be rough, are you planning to have kids in the next 5 years?

Answer: Indirect

"Larry, I've been so focused on my career and training that I haven't had time to think about it. I don't see that happening in the near future."

Answer: Direct

"No, thank you. One is enough."

Do you have kids?

Answer: Indirect

"Yes, I have two beautiful huskies that act just like children and three major projects going through the teenager stage, which makes 5 kids total. Speaking of projects, this position would be involved with..."

Answer: Direct

Yes, No

BONUS

Unless the interviewer is visibly angered by your indirect answer, keep your spouse's work details to yourself. If your spouse makes too much money, the interview may consider lowballing your offer.

If your spouse makes too little or no money, they may perceive your love choice negatively and an indicator of your decision making ability. Of course, either misplaced opinion has nothing to do with you, it's the interviewers perception; however, why give them a chance to trip over their emotional shoelaces?

Q. What does your spouse do for work, if anything?

Answer:
"Tommy's in the government sector. He's got one of those jobs...if I provided you with details, I'd have to make you disappear (be sure to smile at the same time. Don't be creepy). I'm jealous because he basically makes his own schedule; however, it benefits our family because he flexes around my career. Based on my research, I anticipate this position will have times of the year or projects that require after hours work..is that correct?"

What this says about you?
1. You have tact in redirecting a conversation.
2. You showed genuine interest in the position (you researched).

Similar Ignorant Questions:
1. Who's the breadwinner in the family?
2. How many incomes do you have coming in?
3. I might know your spouse, what company does she work for? (when the inquiry is purposely false)

Q. How old are you?

What they want to see:
Who cares what they want to see? Decide beforehand how you're going to be. Age will arise sooner or later in the formal or informal interview. Frame your answer with less emotion and direct it toward the value of your age (young or old).

Answer:
"You're an intelligent guy. I'm sure you've already guessed my age range by the year I graduated college. But if you really want to know, I'm 54 years young. If your concern is about me being technology savvy, I can show you how I create macros in Microsoft Excel in my sleep, install the security cameras I networked in my garage that's viewable on my phone app (wave your phone in the air), or you and I can go head to head on a game of Call of Duty. Would you prefer the Xbox or Playstation?"

What this says about you?
1. You have a playful competitive nature (battle games).
2. You are clearly the nontraditional 54 year old.

Similar Ignorant Questions:
What year did you graduate college?
How old are your kids?
You seem rather young for the responsibility required for this position?

BONUS: Addressing the interviewers concerns up front, with examples, and extending a polite challenge demonstrates your ability to not be rattled by their illegal or inappropriate questions. This example highlights a technology bias. Other common bias's are: youth, market trends, creative thinking, physical fitness, market wisdom, communication skills, and more.

WRAP IT UP

3 Proven Strategies to Advance past illegal questions:

1. Use closed ended answers and questions when possible.
Answer questions with one word: no, yes, or interesting. Ask questions that require a one word answer to move the conversation beyond unprofessional dialogue.

2. Less is more
No chicken and 'waffles' please. Do not ramble or 'waffle' your answer. Keep it brief, concise, and with a neutral tone (easier said than done if you don't practice)

3. Be Waterford crystal clear
Be intentional with your answer. Know your limits up front: What you're willing to answer, what offends you, or what do you deem a *'50 Shades of Grey'* area? The short answer. Be prepared.

11

Military Muscle

Coming home questions

"Baby, you have to figure out a way to pay for college, because we just don't have the money." After my mom spoke those words, I made a decision. I'd serve four years in the military and the G.I. bill would pay for school. The day before I signed with my Air Force recruiter, Coach John Sauerhage, stepped on our field, introduced himself, and offered me a scholarship. That ended my military career before it started; however, being that I was willing to give four years of my life to serve my country...

I have a deep river pride and infinite gratitude for those who lace up their boots so we can live freedom.

With respect to interviews, I find that my military people are ingrained with strong fundamental skill sets (loyalty, honesty, problem solver, pro-activeness, to name a few). However, when it's time to transition into Civi's (street clothes) and enter corporate America, many of you fail at making simple interview tweaks that will enable you to Rockstar your interview. That changes now. This section will show you how to:

- Develop a One-Minute Resume that demonstrates your major value.
- Deploy a psychological advantage for military women.
- Avoid common corporate interview traps.

Before we begin, understand that although small in numbers, prejudice and negative stereotypes about former military members still exists. It's your mission to disarm silent questions racing around the track inside the interviewer's head:

- Are you a military professional or a jarhead?
- Do you have emotional battle baggage?
- Did you join the military to escape civilian life?
- Are you a creative problem solver or a mere direction taker?
- Do you have a sense of humor or does your face hurt to smile?

- Will you be redeployed and we'll be down another body again?
- Will you be a FMLA (Family Medical Leave Act) nightmare because of some medical condition I can't ask you about?
- Are you a worker's compensation case waiting to happen?

True, these thoughts are unfair and judgmental but they're logical human thoughts and who said life was fair? Think about it. If you're the selected candidate, they'll potentially be spending more time with you than their family on a weekly basis. Therefore, it's only natural to ask...

Will hiring you make my life easier or harder?

Let's get started.

The One-Minute Resume
Short answer: Delivering your work experience in less than 60 seconds.

Long Answer: Briskly walking down your work experience in this format:

Company 1:
Title:
Location:
Length of Time:
Major Learning:

Company 2:
Title:
Location:
Length of Time:
Major Learning:

Continue with each additional position

Here's how it sounds:

"In the Air Force, I was a Construction Inspector in South Carolina for

two years. I inspected flight simulator facilities totaling $13 million and honed my investigator skills. I was promoted to Construction Management Chief and transferred to Kuwait for 18 months, where I supervised 4 inspectors, $27.5 million in property, and sharpened my management talents in the Military Academy and with mentors.

I was promoted once more to Base Civil Engineer in Kuwait. And for 3 years, I managed a team of 100 military personal, 20 civilian contractors, and $67 million in property covering 87 acres. I was awarded Officer of the Month for my contract management and organizational strategy skills. Mike (you're speaking to the interviewer), what else would you like to know?"

Note: Slow down when you deliver the last sentence. This technique pulls your listener in closer and allows them to feel more connected to your background instead of bull-rushed with information.

The one-minute resume does several things:
1. Sets a professional tone for the interview.
2. Gives the interviewer a snap shot of your value to the organization.
3. Immediately separates you from candidates who ramble, stumble, or lack confidence.

Of course, tailor how much detail you provide, according to your life experience.
- More positions...less detail.
- Fewer positions...more detail.
- Highlight experience that aligns with the position your applying for.

The Psychological Advantage of Military Women:
As much as I'd like to express this point in words, this is a conversation. I cover this topic online. Use the special code given to you and log on at: www.rockstaryourinterview.com

If you've stumbled across this book and have not been given the special code, follow the instructions under the "Military" tab at the link above.

Avoid Common Military Mistakes

1. Combat Experience:

Mention the ugly details of war only if you want to risk losing the job. Most interviewers don't care or prefer not to hear war stories for various reasons. They're concerned with the value you bring to them and the organization. Stick to value.

2. Military Terms

Replace 'Battalion' with "Large Organization". Use "Senior Vice President" in place of "Commander" and "Director" instead of "Captain". Don't Say: "I was a MOS 351M / Military Occupational Specialty Personnel". Instead say, "I was a Human Intelligence Technician."

3. Emotion-less

When I was working with a Master Sargent, he had all the skills, knowledge, and experience dreams are made of...but couldn't earn the job he was after. We changed three things, he smiled more, told a couple of personal micro stories, and laughed more. That's it. He got the job. Be human.

4. Recon (Reconnaissance for civilian readers) Not researching the position, company, industry, geography, etc. is unacceptable. Do your Recon or suffer lost points in the interview.

Q. You're used to people following orders, how will you deal with our environment where we constantly challenge your ideas?

What they want to see:
Passive aggressive challenges like this question tests the effrontery of your core traits. As my Marines say, *'adapt and overcome'*. The interviewer wants to see if you'll be able to make a smooth and effective transition from military to corporate life or if you have the skills to do so.

Answer:
"You know what's interesting about following orders? Before orders are given, typically there's plenty of discussion, challenge, and sometimes, confrontation. I embrace challenge. That's how ideas get better; as long as they're are delivered in a respectful manner."

What this says about you:
1. You're no stranger to challenge and it doesn't phase your behavior or performance.
2. Your brief answer is clear and stated as a matter of fact which oozes confidence.

Follow up questions: *(based on this answer)*
1. What would you do if a direct report ignored your order and their decision resulted in a better outcome?
2. What would you do if a direct report lied to you and you found out about it?

Red Flag:
1. If you get defensive or overly emotional in the face of tough interview questions.

2. If you don't have individual answers and resort back to the safe zone of following the chain of command or the policy manual.

Q. What qualities do you look for in a boss?

What they want to see:
I hope you don't pass over this question because you believe the answer to be pure common sense. In short, the interviewer wants to see normalcy with a twist of creativity.

Answer:
"Interesting you ask this question. I used to look for the typical key words: honesty, open communication, good mentor, great leader...those traits are important, but now I look deeper. I look for a supervisor who is absolutely certain about their purpose in the organization. They know their 'why'.

Why the company exists and how their position affects the final product, and I look for trust in my manager to correctly position my talents so I'm using my strengths most of the time."

What this says about you:
1. You've been around the block and look for depth in a supervisor.
2. You exhibit signs of being a thought leader.

Follow up questions: *(based on this answer)*
1. What would be an example of you working with your strengths?
2. How would your performance be affected under an indecisive supervisor?

Red Flag:
1. Being sarcastic with answers like, *"I hope my supervisor has a sense of humor or a clue about what his direct reports do."*

2. Exposing major flaws inside your answer. For example, *"I look for a boss who's a good trainer in case I have trouble picking up any new tasks."* Yes, candidates really do deliver answers like this.

Q. What's your preferred management style?

What they want to see:
This is yet another question where you can be a hero or a zero in a

matter of seconds. The interviewer is looking for a style that embraces the environment of their team, department, or organization. Again, this is why recon is hypercritical. Do your homework.

Answer:
"A direct answer, my preferred management style is autonomous. I love it when my direct reports know their role, creatively accomplish assignments, and bring recommendations or solutions to the table along with the problem. But we live in the real world, don't we?

So, I find my style being 'needs oriented', based on the needs of my people. Indecisive folks need micromanagers, rainmakers need give-me-space managers, and creative people need project managers to keep them on task. Autonomous is preferred, but my people dictate the style I frequently use."

What this says about you:
1. You're a real person with a preference and don't straddle the fence with your answer.
2. You demonstrate a 'situational' management style by showing not saying it.

Follow up questions: *(based on this answer)*
1. What do you do when none of your styles help correct a problem employee's performance?
2. What style are you the most uncomfortable using?

Red Flag:
1. Citing you don't have a preferred style is wishy-washy and negative in the mind of decision makers. Pick two or three styles you can choose from and back them up with situations depending on who you're interviewing with.

2. Having a preferred style and not being able to explain why or how you use it.

Q. Tell me about a time when you were in a personal situation that made you feel insecure?

What they want to see:

This is a great time to tell a micro story and show your future employer you can turn a mess that made you insecure into a success and lesson learned. People connect with polite imperfections. It makes them feel as if you've shared the same experiences.

Answer:
"I was stationed at the San Diego Naval Base, we went swimming in the ocean and I got out a little too far. The current kept pushing me further away from shore. I got scared when my legs cramped and my head went under a couple times. Then, I remember my training, calmed down, floated on my back until my legs got better. It took forever, but I slowly made it back to shore. I felt insecure about my lack of awareness and certainly learned my lesson."

What this says about you:
1. You can express being vulnerable.
2. In stressful situations you can still think effectively.

Follow up questions: *(based on this answer)*
1. What did you do wrong to put you in that situation?
2. Tell me about a time that made you feel insecure at work?

Red Flag:
1. Save Superman for the comic books. If you're going to play the "I'm never insecure role", you'll be one secure jobless fool.

2. A candidate once said he felt insecure about his actions after he, *"received the second sexual harassment complaint."* Really? I'll say it again; you can't make this stuff up. Needless to say, use appropriate insecure examples.

Q. Every job has a learning curve, what do you believe would be the biggest challenge for you in this position?

What they want to see:
Have you done more than just apply for the position? Have you intelligently thought about how your skills would help you transition into the position? Do you know where the potential gaps are between your skills and what you've researched? The interviewer is looking for

responses that convey you've thought about questions similar to these.

Answer:
"Well, I was reviewing the transcripts from the last public meeting...and it seemed like the organization interacts with at least five separate public agencies during large-scale exercises. I'd say the biggest learning curve will be developing relationships and learning the tendencies of the other organizations and the personalities that lead them."

What this says about you:
1. You showed the interviewer you researched facts about the company.
2. You're able to think and answer as if you're already in the position.

Follow up questions: *(based on this answer)*
1. Your predecessor burned several bridges. What's your plan to reestablish territory relationships?
2. What will you do if all your efforts to develop relationships fail?

Red Flag:
1. If you don't have a clear sense of what the potential challenges could be.
2. A great way to score zero points on this question is to admit fault of a basic skill such as a lack of confidence. For example, *"I don't know if I'll be able to handle everything all five agencies do."*

Wrap it up:

Speak With Charm to Burn

1. Be conversational.

Speak like you would at a nice cocktail party, off to the side with a small group of people (without the drinks). Answer honestly and show how your mistakes were viewed as lessons learned. The ability to modestly laugh at yourself shows maturity. Be clear, concise, and weave in a micro-story when appropriate to illustrate your POV (Point of view).

2. Be Likable.

A millionaire executive recently told me, *"when I interview anyone, I'll look down for an extended moment and quickly glance up to see their 'true' expression."* Make strong eye contact with your interviewer(s) and practice a natural smile or soft "I'm enjoying this even though I'm dying inside" expression. Especially, when you make a mistake.

3. Be YOU

To be a confident 'you', become familiar with who you are: Emotional triggers, pet peeves, unique quirks, and be in love with exactly who you are at this moment. 1. You're not going to change it before the interview. 2. If you don't fall in love with yourself, how can your interviewer fall in love with your answers? Charm begins within.

Frequency + Exposure = Confidence.

12

Trouble in Paradise

Mental Toughness and Judgment questions

The 'no correct answer' questions are advanced tests. The interviewer is looking for additional evidence that you'll be able to handle gray area situations. They are less concerned with your answer and more concerned with your reasoning, intent, and the 'why' behind your answer. And of course, they want to see how you respond under micro pressure, how you organize thoughts, and if you can deliver a brief, yet reasonable answer.

"Don't wish for easier situations, develop better skills."

The mental toughness you show by answering the question asked, with a logical approach, and without getting visually flustered will determine whether the interviewer can picture you walking around their office...or not.

Let's go.

Q. What would you do if someone continuously took credit for your great ideas? What if that someone was your boss?

What they want to see:
Again, there's no right or wrong answer here. However, there is a good and less than good answer. Your level of tact, ego, and backbone are all on trial. Give the jury an answer resembling:

Answer:
"Unfortunately, I've had this happen to me with a coworker who I was close with. I'd often share my innovative ideas with Jane during lunch before department meetings. She acted like a soundboard and would play devil's advocate to test my views from various angles.

Before I'd get a chance to present my idea, our manager would announce his ideas first and they always seemed to be exactly like mine.

After the third time, I stopped sharing my ideas with Jane at lunch and sure enough, the coincidences stopped. Jane later asked, "Why don't you let me be your soundboard anymore?" I decided a crucial conversation was in order.

I said, "Three times I shared great ideas with you and later, Mark seemed to have the same idea in our meetings. When I stopped sharing, he stopped having identical ideas as me. What are your thoughts on that?" She initially denied it, I remained silent, she later confessed and apologized. I didn't hold a grudge; however, didn't share my best ideas with her."

PART TWO Answer:

"I haven't had a boss take credit for my work before. But if it did happen, I would treat it differently because I believe I'm there to make my boss look good. Let's say it did happened and my boss acknowledged me privately and on my reviews, I probably wouldn't address it.

If my boss didn't acknowledge my work and I wasn't being rewarded for it, I would have a conversation during my review or request a private meeting to discuss my observations. I'd use the word observations, not concerns, to remove as much emotion as possible and speak objectively."

What this says about you:
1. You have a backbone and stand up for yourself.
2. You have conflict resolution skills.
3.. You take action instead of ignore situations.

Follow up Questions: (based on this answer)
1. Under what circumstances would you trust Jane again?
2. What would you do if your boss blew off your concerns after your meeting?

Red Flags:

1. Talking bad about someone as a person for having a moment of bad judgment.
2. Getting overly emotional or ducking your head in the sand to ignore an akward situation.

Q. If there was a talented staff member who confided in you that he was interviewing to leave the company, as a manager what would you do, if anything?

What they want to see:
When there are conflicting loyalties, how do you choose and why? The interviewer is looking for the reasons 'why' and motivation behind the decision you're about to convey.

Answer:
"When I was at Allied financial, I had a great mentor who was preparing me for a regional manager position. My coworker and friend, James, didn't feel as fortunate. He was frustrated about the opportunities Douglas, my mentor, was giving me and didn't want to get left behind.

I knew James lived in the gym and asked him to help me lose some weight. When he was killing me during a workout, I asked, "I know you're frustrated, but what would make you stay?" He told me, "Tom's not grooming me like Douglas is grooming you. If Tom can't recognized my value, I'm out of here."

After listening, I said, "James, let's make a deal. I'll share all my teachings from Douglas with you after each session and introduce you to my outside think tank of executives I have once a month." He asked what my angle was.

I said, "You have to stay on and give your direct reports exactly what you're missing from Tom." He asked again, "What's in it for you?" I said, "1. We're friends, and 2. Your ideas inspire me. And I don't want to lose either." He agreed to stay for two months. After four months; unfortunately, Tom still didn't notice James's efforts but the Vice President did and asked James to be his mentee."

What this says about you:
1. You take action that benefit the company.
2. You understand the value of relationships and loyalty.
3. You know how to ethically exercise influence.

Follow up Questions: *(based on this answer)*

1. What would you have done if James didn't agree and kept interviewing?

2. What type of situation would make you disclose an employee's confidential conversation with you?

Red Flag:

1. Not taking action to save a good employee, *"it's his problem, not mine"* attitude.

2. Breaking confidence to look good in front of your supervisor or others.

BONUS

Some companies will ask you to meet with an in house psychologist who will ask multiple, similar, and emotional based questions. This is another test of your mental toughness and emotional intelligence. Remember to breathe, know the words and phrases that trigger fear in you, and practice being consistent with your answers (tone and delivery).

Q. Have you ever fired a direct report? Why?

What they want to see:

If you're interviewing for a position with direct reports, the interviewer wants to know if you've been exposed to tough emotional situations. They also want to check in with your level of tact.

Answer:

"Unfortunately, yes, I fired a direct report for continually falling short of his productivity targets. He was on a P.I.P. (performance improvement plan) for 3 months after we identified his core issue. It was activity ratios.

He was charismatic; however, not very technical. And when our new products focused more on technical value, he procrastinated booking prospect appointments in fear of being embarrassed because of his lack of knowledge.

Less appointments equaled low ratios, equaled low statistical performance. He was plenty confident, just not competent. After analyzing the costs, I wasn't willing to invest more time in his improvement at the expense of the attention needed for my other direct reports."

What this says about you:
1. You are familiar with improvement plans.
2. You terminate with facts, not with emotion.
3. You separate performance vs. personality.

NOTE: Be prepared to discuss your specific actions, resources provided, and follow-up procedures with respect to the personal improvement plan (PIP).

Follow up Questions: *(based on this answer)*
1. Would you walk me through the framework of your last PIP plan?
2. Exactly what 'costs' did you analyze?

Red Flags:
1. If it becomes clear you actually did not provide your direct report with a fighting chance to improve.
2. If you talk poorly of your direct report using emotional words (i.e., stupid, fool, crazy, lazy, etc.) vs. facts and stats.

Q. How many cigars are smoked in a year? *(Out of Bounds Questions)*

What they want to see:
If this question seems odd, it is. Someone, somewhere was attempting to be unique and they succeeded. The question tests your awareness of global, regional, and demographic statistics in addition to 'on your feet' math skills simultaneously. Your goal is to logically walk your audience through the steps from question to answer.

Answer:

"Let's see, there are roughly 300 million people in the U.S.. To make the math easy, let's say 50% are men. That's 150 million. And if 60% of men are above the age of 25, now we're at 90 million. And the last research I recall showed one in every ten men smoke, bringing us to 9 million. Again, let's assume only 5% of smokers are cigar smokers. Now, we're at roughly 450,000. If all of them smoked once a week, that makes around 23 million cigars smoked in a year. Of course, that number needs to be adjusted for accurate data and the few women who smoke cigars."

What this says about you:

1. You can construct a logical answer to an 'outer-space' question.
2. You have solid mental math skills.
3. You have a general knowledge on national statistics and research.

Red Flags:

1. Having no answer or having a weak logical process.
2. Making a joke to cover up your lack of having a Mental 6 Pack.

Q. How do you set and manage goals? And what do you do when you don't reach them?

What they want to see:

How much persistence you have? Are you resilient? Are you organized? Do you have short-term vision, long-term vision, or both? This is the dialogue in the truth seeker's (the interviewer's) mind.

Answer:

"I like the way the author, Stephen Covey, phrases it, 'Begin with the end in mind'. When I set goals, I get a crystal-clear picture of where the finish line is, gauge the type of resources it will take to get there, the environment I'm in, and then reverse engineer the timeline from the end to where I stand now. There are other factors, but that gives you the gist of my flexible framework.

At my previous company, I had to perform a complex property analysis and had 2 weeks to complete it. I used the framework I mentioned and started the project on time but ran into a hiccup after week 1. There was crucial financial data I needed from a business partner but was unaware they were closed for 3 days the following week.

When they returned, I had to scramble to get the information and my project was a day late. In addition, my oversight caused a huge amount of unnecessary stress for my team and me. I guaranteed a mistake like that would never happen again because I added a resource awareness principle to my framework. If I miss a target goal, I assess where the breakdown occurred to prevent it from happening again."

What this says about you:
1. You are familiar with success and management literature.
2. You accept accountability for your actions and acknowledge errors.
3. You implement protocols to avoid repeating mistakes.

Follow up Questions: *(based on this answer)*
1. At what exact point did you know your project would be late?
2. What did you say to your team after the project was complete?

Red Flags:
1. If you blame the company for being closed or your team member's skills for not being able to handle the condensed time line.
2. If you claim to always reach your goals.

Q. In this position, you'll see your boss only once per week. Tell me specifically, how you handle working with little supervision. And how you stayed motivated.

What they want to see:
Am I going to have to babysit you? Can you take minimal direction and run with it? The interviewer is assessing the additional work you're going to be outside of initial training. It's up to you to make them feel like you'll be a turn-key employee.

Answer:
"At my previous company, we experienced a layoff. With less staff I went from seeing my boss 3 full days per week to 4 hours per week. The sudden change was frustrating for both of us - important details were falling through the cracks left and right. I saw Larry and said, "Can we talk? This is crazy." We met for three straight Saturday's...non-paid, and

frame-worked a communication and project flow chart. Most but not all of our problems were solved. Since then, 'little supervision' strategies are hard wired in my brain.

1. We created a shared project flow chart online to see progress remotely.
2. I kept a log of questions, concerns, and innovative ideas to discuss at meetings.
3. We had shared access to each other's work calendars.
4. And we had a 10-minute phone meeting every Monday, Wednesday, Friday until we got help.

Motivation wasn't an issue because I'm a bit of a perfectionist. When I felt run down, I'd make sure to get more sleep, watch what I ate, or hit the gym to get out of my funk."

What this says about you:
1. You're no stranger to doing more with less.
2. You're willing to confront difficult situations.
3. You work for more than just a paycheck (non-paid Saturdays).

Follow up Questions: (based on this answer)
1. What would you have done if Larry blew off your request to talk?
2. What are the two most important qualities to you in a supervisor?

Red Flags:

1. If you would not have been proactive in this or a similar situation allowing the issue to escalate and eventually explode.

2. Holding a grudge or not accepting fault in a 'lack of communication' situation is not a desired character trait.

Q. How many basketballs would it take to fill this room?

What they want to see:
A similar answer as the cigar question on page 120.

Answer:
"Hmmm, this room looks to be 20*10*8. That's 1,600 for the volume. Basketballs are about 10 inches across. Converting 10inches to fit into

one cubic foot, because I'm guesstimating the room in square feet, that's a ratio of about .83...divide that into 1600 and you could put almost 2,000 basketballs in this room. Normal size inflated basketballs that is."

What this says about you:
1. You show quick mental math skills.
2. You have a basic awareness of open space and geometry.
3. You can visualize things you can't see. (a dynamic future-trend trait)

Red Flags:
1. Showing bad body language as if the question irritates you.
2. Passing on the question or not even trying to answer.

Q. Do you prefer to work by yourself or with others? And don't straddle the fence on this answer like everyone else.

What they want to see:
Inside this question, the interviewer is tossing you extra rope and a key. You can verbally hang yourself or open the door to being placed in the 'good candidate' pile. She's telling you in an indirect way: don't waste my time, be original, and answer the damn question.

Answer:
"Judy, I do have a preference...depending on the situation. Earlier this year, I had a medium sized project that involved a lot of creative aspects with floor plans, architectural, and interior design. We had a generous timeline and the creative aspects, although interesting for me, aren't my strengths...so I love to work as a team in this type of environment. I'm good at keeping creative talent on deadlines, without upsetting their egos.

Now, when it came to financing the project, the deadline was much tighter. Forecasting, trending, and juggling the numbers is my strength; therefore, I prefer to work alone and have my boss proof my final proposal. The beauty of working alone is being able to wake up at 2am with an idea and execute vs. wait to get input in the office after the creativity dies. No straddling the fence here."

What this says about you:
1. You understand your strengths and in which situations to use them.
2. You have a flexible personality (focus creative people and you can be independently focused).

Follow up Questions: *(based on this answer)*
1. We have a lot of 'creative egos' here. How exactly do you hold them accountable?
2. What do you do when you're working independently and find that you actually need group input?

Red Flags:
1. If you disregard the interviewer's warning and straddle the fence on your answer.
2. Kiss the job good bye if you don't know your own talents and how to deploy them in simple situations like this.

Wrap it up:

1. University Y.O.U.
The more you understand and can illustrate your value, the easier it will be to handle ambiguous questions with grace.

2. Logic
Break down the 'How many basketballs' type questions in a logical fashion. It's okay to talk your way through an answer verbally. That's exactly what they want to see...the conversation in your head and if your method matches how they run business.

3. Be a Decision Maker
Are you the type of person that asks me where I want to eat vs. telling me your preference? If so, please review this chapter and practice answering the questions with a brutally honest, impatient, decision making 'bully-ish' type friend. Have them critique your responses.

4. Don't Be Perfect
Own your mistakes, illustrate what you learned, and convey what safety nets you put in place to ensure you don't step in the same puddle twice.

5. Personality vs. Commodity
The more you can demonstrate that you're unique, you think differently, you have an uncommon combination of technical and interpersonal skills, the more you're considered a personality vs. a commodity. Personalities can't be replaced or found as easily as commodity candidates. Don't believe me, ask any $250,000+ executive you know.

13

Reverse Engineering

What the interviewer sees

A friend of mine named, Daniel Burrus, wrote the book, *Flash Foresight*. In it, he shows how to use today's data to forecast future events; thereby, solving problems before they arise. Or getting in position today to take advantage of future opportunities before others recognize their existence.

On pg. 144, of Flash Foresight, he uses a concept called Go Opposite. The concept is simple and we'll use it here as an additional tool to Rockstar your interview. One of the best ways to become a better interviewee is to learn how to be a great interviewer (to go opposite). An executive I recently coached in preparation for her interview said this:

> *"Looking back, I wish I would have thought to practice being the interviewer sooner...I might have gotten the last job I interviewed for."*

This chapter is themed reverse engineering because we are Going Opposite to slingshot forward into fiercer interview-based skills. When you master the motivation and practical psychology behind how to be a great interviewer, you naturally become more aware of how to Rockstar your own interview.

Just as I coach up candidates to Rockstar their interview, I also coach executives on identifying Rockstars in the interview...and faux Rockstars. Do you believe this approach will help increase your breath of knowledge and confidence for your interview?

Up to this point, the questions we've been analyzing are from various industries that you may not think relate to your field of expertise. **Do not keep an open mind.** Do not pay attention to the reverse psychology in the previous sentence. Really understand why each question is asked and think, "*how can the concept help me and transfer into my profession?*"

Again, this book is about teaching you **how to answer any question** *asked, not how to memorize answers to questions.*

Shall we begin?

Q. Share with me your quality ratios: in general, how many prospects do you see before closing a sale?

Why this question?

When salespeople are focused on a daily rhythm, it's a direct indicator of long-term success. Car dealerships, restaurants, retail stores, and grocery stores all have daily sales quotas. A quality sales professional will quickly identify and articulate the daily activity it takes to reach her monthly production target.

This is the exact information you want to know from the candidate sitting in front of you. In any sales interview, you must talk about quality ratios when gauging someone's productivity levels *or* you will not have an accurate picture of their true value.

The analysis:

Listen for the candidate's ability or inability to quickly and clearly demonstrate how their daily activity affects their monthly, quarterly, and annual sales targets.

Red Flag:

Beware of candidates who use too many words to explain simple quality ratios, those who cannot articulate a quality ratio, and those individuals who are not able to compute ratios on the spot.

A person who is comfortable and experienced with ratios can calculate quickly, even if they have poor math skills. Why? Because they work with these ratios daily.

Rockstar answer:

"The cost of our synthetic kidneys is between $19,000 and $37,000 wholesale. I need to sell .5 units per week or 2 units per month to meet my sales goal. My demonstration-to-sale ratio is 35 to 1 so that means I have to demonstrate our product a minimum of 70 times each month or 4 times per day. When my ratios are met, my sales almost always follow

suit."

Q. What was your favorite position and how did your boss play a role in making it unique?

Why This Question?
This question invites any person to reflect on positive situations from the past that are full of passionate memories. It is what I call a slow pitch softball question. Give the candidate something easy to answer that makes them smile and lower their defensive shields. Your job is to look for the subtle clues, micro expressions, in search for the truth.

The Analysis:
A savvy CEO and recruiters will tell you how this question sets the stage. The candidates body language will soften, their breathing pattern will become more relaxed, and their eyes will open wider because of the pleasant memories they're ruminating over. In this state you're able to prep the candidate to have a more natural response to upcoming questions that challenge their pedigree.

Red Flag:
Take a look at the pharmaceutical sales rep named Candace. When she answered this question, she made the mistake of mentioning a previous position where she enjoyed being outdoors, fast paced office visits, and dinners with prospective clients.

True, she was interviewing for a pharmaceutical sales position; however, **it was a managerial position.**

Candace was up selling her love for a fast-paced environment and the company's position didn't match her passionate description. Fifty percent of her time would be spent alone forecasting sales, analyzing trends, and charting employee development plans.

Her answer betrayed her chances of earning the position. The company was not able to offer her the regular experience of engaging with clients on a consistent basis. Therefore, she was deemed not a good fit for the office-type environment required of managers at the company.

Q. What position did you like the least and what factor did your boss play in that situation?

Why This Question:
When a candidate is presented with an opportunity to throw stones at her former boss or company, be hyperaware of the micro facial expressions and change in body language. This question is a perfect opportunity for complainers to step forward and be known.

The Rockstar candidate response accepts responsibility for past actions and avoids thrusting bad experiences on others or playing the blame game. In addition, look for the candidate's ability to be objective and separate their emotion when illustrating the situation.

The Analysis:
You get to see how the candidate articulates an uncomfortable memory, takes responsibility for the part they played or not, and recommend future actions that will prevent similar occurrences.

Red Flag:
Candidates are typically on their best behavior when they interview. If she complains even slightly, how much will she complain after she passes probation?

Rockstar Answer:
Listen for deep listening inside the answer. Does the candidate's character and personality traits align with your company culture, your team, and with you? Here's an example of how a positive response may sound.

"To be direct, my least favorite position was working for Debbie, my boss at Petro. She didn't prepare for the shift from traditional based marketing to online strategic marketing. As a result our company experienced a steady downward trend in web traffic. When I'd bring web based ideas to the table, I would be shot down; however, still held accountable for website traffic and ROI goals.

I showed her research from our competitor's models and similar industries we could test at minimal cost. I even asked a coworker to present my idea, in case it was something about me. Still, no luck. Not feeling supported by my boss made it hard to come to work each day. After 9 months of declined proposals, I accepted an offer after being recruited at a trade show."

Q. What are the 2 most common objections you face, and how do you handle them?

Why this question?
Typically, in any given industry, there are no more than 4-7 common objections industry professionals face. This question is important because you get to hear how the candidate responds on the spot.

They have an audience, you, there are no do overs, and you get to see how comfortable the candidate is at being uncomfortable. This micro role-play will provide you specific insights on the candidate's content delivery, creativity, and verbal sophistication.

The analysis:
You have already painted the 1st strokes over the analysis canvas. Now is the time for acute observation. What does that mean exactly? When the candidate responds to this question, observe how easily and fluidly she delivers the information. Does she have to think about her answer? Is she stumbling over her words? Will she look you straight in the eye? Did she answer with a confident tone? Do you get the feeling that she's comfortable talking about objections?

Red Flag:
The power to develop relationships quickly and exercise strategic influence are critical tools in establishing new accounts. If his answer to objections sounds like every other candidate you've interviewed, you're not speaking with a future employee.

Beware of ordinary answers such as, *"I can guarantee you a price match if...,"* *"Our features are far superior to your current provider because...,* or *"You've been with the same company for 7 years, let me show you how our company is on the cutting edge and..."*

Rockstar answer:
Look for candidates who respond with creative insights and position common sense information in creative angles that touch on the emotion

of a potential client. Think how a potential hedge fund manager with an economics degree might respond to the objection, *"I've been working with my current financial institution for 11 years and we're close friends."*

Rockstar Role Play:

"Jim, relationships are what I respect most in my professional and personal life. My only suggestion to you is to use my services in special or unique situations. I'm confident you know there are occasions when you need to use an outsider. I'm a unique breed with a Master's in international economics and I can help clients see financial opportunities before they reach the States.

Again, I don't expect you to abandon an 11-year friendship because I'm on your doorstep. But, I would like your permission to share information on how I identify these financial windows before they appear. A great number of attorneys depend on my forecasts to stay ahead of the competition. I've been successful creating investment strategies on the front end of the opportunity life cycle and the backend. Does that sound like something that could be of value to you?"

Q. What's changed in your situation since the last time we spoke?

Why this question?

By now, you have already calculated how expensive it is to recruit candidates. This is your opportunity to further save money, time, energy, and resources by providing the candidate one last chance to back out or share unexpected circumstances. This is what legal council calls a due diligence question.

The analysis:

7 out of 10 times, the candidate will say nothing has changed. With that said, you just effectively soft closed your new employee and have the green light to move to the next step.

Conversely, if something has changed like a counter offer from his current company, a competing job offer, or any type of unexpected personal decision, then you must quickly assess the situation. Find out exactly what's changed and, on a scale of 1 to 5, how seriously has the change altered the interest in this position for the candidate.

Red Flag:
Be aware of candidates who take a long time to make a decision. Most likely, you have gone through multiple rounds of interviews already and the candidate has had ample opportunity to interview your company and you during the process. After an offer has been made, taking up to 24-hours to think about the decision is normal. Multiple days to make a decision is unacceptable (Yes, there are exceptions).

Candidates who take long periods of time to make a decision are stalling for a reason. They could be waiting for an alternate company's offer, currently involved in the final stages of another interview process, or various other reasons. The fact remains, the candidate does not display the ability to make a decision.

Think to yourself. Is this the type of person that you want to work for your organization? Again, there are exceptions to every rule. Only you know when it's acceptable for any one candidate to be allowed more than 24 hours to make a decision.

Rockstar Answer:
"The only thing that's changed is my level of excitement. This position seems like a perfect fit."

Q. When do you disagree with your boss the most? And tell me how you handled the last time she was wrong and you were right?

Why this question?
Have you heard the saying, "Opinions are inevitable but conflict is optional?" That sounds nice in theory but in practice, conflict is a commonplace in the workplace. It can be challenging to observe a candidate's propensity to handle conflict. On one hand, you want an employee with a backbone. On the other hand, you don't want a bully on your team.

It's understandable that the candidate may be nervous answering this question, but that's okay. This gives you further insight if the candidate is able to **be comfortable being uncomfortable**. During this answer, pay close attention if the candidate can take responsibility for his actions. Also, note if this situation changed the dynamics of the relationship between the candidate and his boss. More specifically, does this candidate hold grudges?

The analysis:
This answer requires you to brush up on your psychology 101 notes. Do they speak about the situation with heavy emotion or do they address it as if it's an everyday conversation? Do they have a noticeable shift in posture? Does the pitch of their voice change? Your goal is to determine what types of issues rise to the level of conflict worthy. Also, are the conflicts technical in nature, interpersonal, or environmentally driven? Finally, how does all this data match up with you and your organization?

Red Flag:
Study how the candidate deals with their bosses feelings after the conflict is resolved. Phrases we don't want to hear sound like, "*my boss knew I was right but wouldn't admit it,*" "*It was obvious she was not on top of her game,*" or "*I usually come out on top when we disagree.*" Listen closely for micro-signs of gloating, arrogance, and the general lack of emotional intelligence. You probably have more than your fair share of mental vagabonds at your organization and this is a perfect opportunity to guard against hiring one more.

Rockstar answer:
The end result for you is to identify candidates who complement the weaknesses of the department, remain objective when expressing their opinion, and are able to move forward without spreading conflict residue when it has ended. A solid answer will sound something like:

"Jerry and I challenge each other mostly on timing issues. Specifically, when to role out protocol in a sales cycle. On our last product launch, he wanted to deliver to our VIP companies before training sales staff. I agreed that our VIP clients should have first touch, but wanted the sales force to be trained first to handle user questions effectively.

My solution was the correct action to take, but that's only because I focus more on the technical aspects and he focuses on the strategic and visionary aspects. I was less concerned about who was right or wrong and more concerned with my boss looking competent when presenting test results to our VP.

I don't see our conflict as conflict, it's more of a checks and balance system...there are many times when he's right and I'm wrong."

Q. On a scale of 1 to 10, how would you rate your ability to predict situations before they occur? Specifically, how would you rate your intuition, timing, and proactive nature on the job?

Why this question?
One of the most critical skills for an employee in a fast paced environment is the ability to see problems before they roll around the corner. You're looking for the uncanny ability of an individual to understand other people's roles responsibilities and timelines in conjunction with their own. A office quarterback mindset, if you will.

The analysis:
You already know a quality candidate will have a story ready to demonstrate their skill and savvy. That's why you must use a behavioral interview method to squeeze out additional information which speaks to the candidate's core characteristics.

Use follow-up questions like, *"Give me an example when a project was so large you feared the initial deadline would not be met. What did you see that made you feel that way?"* or *"Tell me about a recent experience where you made a serious miscalculation on a tight project timeline. When exactly did you know you were in the danger zone?"*

Red flag:
Your head should spin off your body faster than a hungry owl in a laboratory of 1,000 wild mice if you hear answers that sound like:

"I don't know how to rate this question, I've never been blindsided..."
"I always finish projects on time because I catch every problem..."
"I'm a 9 out of 10. I'd be a 10 if everyone else would pull their weight..."

Rockstar answer:

"I believe I'm good at predicting situations before they occur, both opportunities and problems. Last year, I accepted a newly created position at my company. My first mission was to centralize 4 separate departments' marketing budgets totaling $325,000. Surprisingly, there were very few procedures in place qualifying the needs for media purchases, travel, and equipment expenditures.

After my first couple of days, I could see where the frustration, competition for dollars, and personality conflicts ignited because of the lack of standardization. Each department thought their way was best.

After asking for each department's wish list, within four months and the help from I.T., I created an intranet portal that standardized the procedures and captured the information for media purchases, travel, and equipment expenditures. I rate myself an 8 for this question because there's always room for improvement."

Bonus:

Even though some answers sound good on the surface, dig deeper with follow-up questions like:

"Did you receive recognition after your 4 month project ended? If so what type of recognition and from whom?"

"You mentioned personality conflict and frustration, give me an example of a situation you encountered and how you handled it?"

Creating a centralized system is a solid accomplishment. But what we really want to know is how did the executives and other decision-makers in the company appreciate the end result. Did these bottom-line-dollar thinkers perceive the project as valuable to the organization? That's one of the main reasons to peal back the layers of the interview onion.

Q. What skills do you need to improve upon in the next year?

Why this question:

All high performers have the ability to be self-critical and self analyze frequently. Without a built-in internal checks and balance system, a candidate may require a great deal of hand holding to recognize his shortcomings.

On the other hand, when candidates transparently speak of their weaknesses from an objective point of view, it's a lesser challenge to correct mistakes as they occur. In this situation, the organization is more concerned with providing the necessary structure and resources to the employee rather than overseeing his behavior.

The analysis:
Listen for candidates to express both short and long-term goals. The short-term addressing immediate needs, skill gaps and long term geared toward the framework of a person's career and a strategic road map to the finish line.

A Hollywood video editor might focus, in the short term, on the technical aspect of mastering a new software program. In contrast, a long-term goal may be rooted in the study of leadership and conflict resolution skills, in hopes of one day being a Director.

Red Flag:
When you receive a canned response such as, "*I need to work on my time management skills, because I'm a workaholic who rarely takes breaks and lunches.*" Your BS Meter should activate. You should also be leery of individuals who openly destroy their candidacy citing answers such as, "*I need to work on my patience and delegation abilities.*"

And "*When it's crunch time, I tend to get cranky and finish my direct reports' work if they don't take action quickly enough.*" You're watching for the right balance of openness to critique one's self, the ability to identify real weaknesses, and provide solutions that overcome behavioral hurdles.

Rockstar answer:
"*Even though I'm a top producer, my monthly averages for new business development were sporadic. There were times when I would hyper focus on turning prospects into clients and closing the sale to the degree that my new-business generation activities would suffer.*

When preparing for my annual review, I identified 2 areas of improvement. One, to become more proficient with our client tracking software; thereby saving time, specifically, an additional 45 minutes/day. Two, pre-plan new business activities and strategize 4 months out to save an additional 2 hours/week."

Q. What makes you stand out among your co-workers?

Why this question?

The simplicity of this question is often underestimated until the overconfident or unprepared candidate opens his mouth. The first section of this book concentrated on remembering who you are as an individual such as, what skills, talents, and traits you hold and how those tools can be transformed into value for a potential employer.

This question tests your ingenuity of taking your skill-ingredients, mixing them together, and delivering a clear, value driven answer based on the organization's needs.

The Analysis:

When asking this question, you'll elicit a mixed bag of answers:

- *"I'm not sure"*
- *"It's my personality, work ethic"*
- *"Nobody works longer hours than I do"*

And more content-based answers such as:

- *"I created a market survey, and identified a new niche customer that brought an additional 3% revenue margin."*

Of course, with content brings dialogue. You'll squeeze more juice out of the question with follow-ups:

- *"What type of survey did you conduct and how did you identify the sample participants?"*
- *"What exactly made you take action on your survey idea?"*
- *"How did you get approval?"*

Red Flag:

Fact or Fiction? Although it may be nice to hear a candidate bring home the moon and stars in a content-based answer, how accurate is it and is it what your company needs? Is it what you need? Not every position you interview for requires a hot shot employee eager to put the company on the cover of Fortune Magazine.

If a candidate tries to over impress you with similar answers or pulls back with, "*Interesting, I'm not sure...,*" that sets the tone for the rest of the interview. Be prepared to probe further and extract the pacifier from the interviewer-newborn.

Rockstar Answer:
"Well, during my last review, Ken, my boss told me he really appreciated three things I do extraordinarily well. 1. Whenever I bring problems to his attention, I offer potential solutions even if I have to research an unknown topic. 2. I stay unusually calm when our VP has fits of yelling when disseminating or requesting time sensitive information.

And 3., he appreciates how I teach my coworkers the skills, information, or processes I research and learn on my own time. He says it saves him time from having to do it. I didn't realize he appreciated it so much until he told me, but I'm just acting how I'd want and expect my direct reports to act. He didn't say it directly, but I got the feeling these three things made me stand out from my peers."

BONUS:
When listening to these answers, think Psychology 101. See if you're able to reverse engineer what type of environment this individual derives from. And will his background be a fit with your team?

Q. In general, how lucky would you say you are in your professional career?

Why ask this question?
Because it tells you about the core belief of the person you're speaking with. Today's experts have finally proven, scientifically, that every thought creates a physical response in the body. Specifically, the release of hormones. For example, a stressful thought releases cortisol, and a happy thought releases dopamine.

Further studies show how these hormones are tied to levels of productivity, sickness, and accuracy. This question is critical when understanding what the candidate thinks about when conflict arises and to be cognizant of their predominant mindset.

The Analysis:

When interviewing for an executive position over six figures, I had a candidate say,

"I wouldn't have any luck if it wasn't for bad luck."

Is this the mindset you want leading 1,500 employees in 3 states? Probably not. What about the Director of Risk Management or the Director of Emergency Management? Possibly.

Just as aggressively optimistic belief systems have their place in leadership roles, so too do pessimistic mentalities. This question quickly identifies the candidate's true colors. It's up to you to understand if they match the colors of your organization's outfit and your position's functions and roles.

Red Flag:

Statements like:

"All buyers are liars," "You can't trust employees further than you can throw them," or "It doesn't matter, it will never work" are all red flag answers.

There are pessimists who are factual rather than emotional. They view their belief as a protection device. As previously stated, this type of 'devil's advocate' approach can be useful in specific roles; however, the tone an delivery must be neutral in order for this type of personality to be effective long term.

Rockstar Answer:

"Using a scale of 1-10, I'd have to say I'm an 8 and sometimes 9 when it *comes to being lucky. When I have unmanageable deadlines, get frustrated, or identify financial signals that don't look promising, something always happens to turn the situation around and save the day. For instance, last December, it was clear we weren't going to make our year-end totals; some of my team even canceled vacations because they depended on their bonus'.*

I asked everyone to call on each other's cold accounts, thinking a new voice may revitalize some business. They groaned because we were 17% out from goal. And guess what? Jamie struck gold. She contacted a client who Jack had misfiled and that one account was 11% of the 17% needed. Everyone's excitement in the office created the 'hustle bug' and pushed us over goal. It was lightening in a bottle."

Wrap it up:

1. What's in it for me?

Write down at least two things you learned acting like you're on the other side of the table. And how does that change your presentation style, content, and delivery?

2. Practical Psychology

Practice creating interview questions for the position you're currently in. Understand the 'why' behind your question. What's the end result you're most concerned with. Use practical psychology to quickly understand the main concern the interviewer may have and frame your answer to resolve the concern.

3. Practice

Actor, Will Smith said, *"Talent you have naturally. Skill is only developed by hours and hours...of beating on your craft."* Formal and informal interviewing is a craft. Practice daily if you want to be successful at Rock Starring your interviews (formal and informal)

4. Transfer

When you discover a new tool that works, look for other ways to incorporate it into other areas of your life. If 'Going Opposite' helps with interviewing, where else could Going Opposite add value to your life?

5. Video

When practicing your interviewing craft, video tape it. Review the footage, remove distractions, and highlight strong phrases/sentences. Continuously refine your answers for clarity.

14

Every *Body* is in Sales

World Class sales questions

To this day, I'm still amazed how many bachelor degreed, PHD'd, and JD/MD'd candidates go into interviews unprepared to sell their most prized skills according to the questions asked. I'm less concerned why and would rather focus on the solution. In doing so, let's see what tools the pharmaceutical sales rep recruitment process can share with us.

"I'm not lazy,
I just rest before I get tired."

I hope you've been taking notes as you read. Creative ideas will go find someone else to take them seriously if you don't write them down. Pay extra attention to the "**What they want to see**" section. Regardless of the industry, the dialogue inside an interviewers head is surprisingly similar.

Let's go make a sale.

Q. In your opinion, what's the most challenging aspect for a pharmaceutical sales representative?

What they want to see:
Do you have an understanding of the typical challenges (physician access, wicked competition, cost issues, and rejection)? Does your personality and mentality appear to be durable and equipped for the long-term challenge of results performance and a fast pace environment?

Answer:
"I belong to a couple of think tank groups on Linked-In that address problems and solutions for pharm reps. Over the last nine months, it appears that the number one challenge and skill to develop is the ability to build Teflon relationships. Next, is turning objections into solutions.

Mastering how to quickly build relationships is critical for cold calls, turning Lieutenant Dan at the front desk into a friend, standing out from other reps lined up against the wall, and addressing cost concerns with the Dr. I've read the book, How to Win Friends and Influence People, at least four times.

One of several skills I'd employ is keeping a relationship journal that had notes on the main players in each office: names, birthdays, kids, likes, dislikes, sports teams, favorite foods, etc. I'd always show up with valuable information, small personal gifts, not just food. It's hard not to like people who take the time to remember what's important to you. Would you agree?"

What this says about you:
1. You've been researching for nine months.
2. You understand the philosophy of being unique.

Follow up questions: *(Based on this answer)*
1. Tell me more about making Lieutenant Dan your friend...exactly how would you do that?
2. What do you believe are some of the 'cost' issues you'll encounter and how do you propose to overcome them?

Red Flags:
1. If you're not able to show you've researched the position or industry
2. Please **don't** ask about or act excited about the perks, Dr. dinners, company car, or delivering donuts to staff. Be passionate about helping people solving problems and living a higher quality of life vs. one pervaded with pain.

Q. What's your greatest weakness? An honest one, please.

What they want to see:
"C'mon, give up the goods", is what they're thinking. They want to see how you manage around your imperfections. So, show them.

Answer:
"That's easy. My greatest weakness is mundane paperwork. Don't get me wrong, I know it's necessary, I'm accurate and timely...I just don't wake up in the morning saying, "Wow, I can't wait to complete my expense report." See, whenever I have a task I'm less than thrilled with, I use a strategy form Marcus Buckingham's book Go Put Your Strengths to Work. I make my weakness a habit and routinely update my expense

reports on Wednesday and Friday mornings so it doesn't become an overwhelming issue at months' end.

Then, I'm able to do what does get my blood pumping like building relationships, sharing information, and meeting weekly quotas. From the outside, it may look like I'm good with paperwork; however, it's certainly not natural for me...it's a learned habit."

What this says about you:
1. You're honest about what you're not passionate about.
2. You have tools to manage around your perceived weaknesses.

Follow up questions: *(Based on this answer)*
1. What other duties about this job are you not passionate about?
2. What would your boss say your greatest weakness is?

Red Flags:
1. Saying you have no weaknesses is your resume's fast track to the trashcan.
2. Showcasing a weakness that should be a major strength for the position (handling stress, being an influencer, speaking in public comfortably).

BONUS:

Tom Rath wrote a book called, How Full Is Your Bucket. One of the major teachings was: After you finish a conversation with someone, do you feel tired or inspired? If you feel inspired increase the frequency of time you spend with that person(s). If you feel tired, do the reverse.

When you interview, do you inspire your interviewers (your audience) or do you make them tired. Equally as important, how do you know?

Q. How would you handle a physician complaining that your drug is too expensive?

What they want to see:

They're not looking for you to be a magician salesperson, but they are looking for your framework to overcome objections and if what you say matches how you say it.

Answer:

"Once I realized that objections are invitations to ask the right questions, my attitude toward them changed dramatically. If one of my clients is complaining about price, it's because I haven't demonstrated enough value or identified his real objection. So, I'd ask probing questions that get to his real concern like, "What should the product do to make it worth the price?" or "Is it only the price or is there another issue as well?" After I determined the core concerns, then I'd address them directly.

During follow up calls, I'd bring the necessary data, studies, and peer-testimonials based on what the core objections were. If price remains the prime resistance, I'd have brief talking points on the superior value and uniqueness of my product vs. the competition, justifying the price. I'm sure I could use my supervisor as a resource as well."

What this says about you:

1. You have a general understanding of selling psychology.
2. You would ask for help if necessary (use supervisor as resource).

Follow up questions: *(Based on this answer)*

1. How would you go about getting peer-testimonials?
2. How long would you spend on this client before giving up on him?

Red Flags:

1. If you demonstrate frustration during this question, the interviewer will think you'd be even worse in the presence of a surly physician.
2. Making over confident statements like you'd use your charisma or persuade the Dr. with your divine influence.

Q. How do you handle the pressure of sales quotas?

What they want to see:
Everyone's not meant for sales. This question invites you to display how you handle the daily pressures of hitting target numbers.

Answer:
"I rely on ratios and planning to alleviate the pressure of quotas. For example, if my goal is 10 sales per month and my ratio of visits to closing a sale is 7 to 1. I need to visit 70 prospects per month or roughly 17 per week.

To take intelligent action, you need a plan. On Sundays, I write down the game plan for the entire week. Every morning, I review what must take place to stay on target. I've learned through trial and error, research, and mentorship; when I plan my work and work my ratio-plan, my quotas get met."

What this says about you:
1. You set goals and plan your work.
2. You learn through multiple conduits.

Follow up questions: *(Based on this answer)*
1. What other ways do you filter the pressure?
2. When's the last time you didn't meet your quota? What happened?

Red Flags:
1. Pharmaceutical managers have been trained that sales are about personality and metrics. If you don't display both in your answer, don't expect a call back.
2. If you don't sound confident or stumble over your words answering this question, good luck next time kiddo.

Q. What things can cause you to get off track at work or lose drive?

What they want to see:
The interviewer is really asking you, how many times per week am I

going to have to babysit your assets? Is your lack of focus going to affect my focus because you're my direct report? Can I trust you without micromanaging you?

Answer:
"Not planning my week or my day would cause me to get off track. That's why I treat my planning time like religion. To get to this point in my career, I've lost my share friends who are now only acquaintances because I'm so focused. My core friends and family know not to call me with anything frivolous during work hours...only emergencies. And checking to see when I can help move furniture is not an emergency.

Once I've completed my daily goals and reviewed my next day's plans, then I'm able to relax, hit the gym, reply to personal calls/emails, or do something outside of work. You know, it's not easy being disciplined but when I'm at the top of the sales leader board each month, that feeling makes all my discipline worth it."

What this says about you:
1. You're willing to allow some relationships to die.
2. You have demonstrated passion for sales (that feeling makes it all worth it).

Follow up questions: *(Based on this answer)*
1. How do you deal with having a bad week numbers wise?
2. What's the last huge professional mistake you made? How'd you handle it and what was the outcome?

Red Flags:
1. If you admit or hint to having severe challenges staying focused when working alone.
2. If you say or act as if you've never had or don't have challenges staying focused...you lose credibility and trust.

Q. What would you do if a competitor hid or moved your samples?

What they want to see:
Unfortunately, when it comes to sales, there will always be dirty players.

How you handle unfair tactics tells what type of savvy you do or don't have.

Answer:
"When by the sample area, I'd ask the doctor if he knows where my product is. If he was unable to easily locate it, I'd mention a top feature of the product and how it would benefit his patients...but only if the product was available.

I'd offer to help and ask him where exactly he'd like my product placed. I believe doctors aren't new to the 'hide the competitor's stash game.' And depending on our relationship, I might ask how many times he's seen product grow feet and hide themselves.

Without pointing fingers or saying anything negative about the competition, I would have addressed the problem to the physician and he'd know where to reach for my product because he selected the sample's location. Again, depending on my favorability, I would ask one of the nurses or office staff to keep an eye out for my magical product samples that relocate themselves mysteriously."

What this says about you:
1. You bring problems forward without whining or complaining.
2. You'd tactfully address the problem with staff as well as the physician.

Follow up questions: *(Based on this answer)*
1. How would you bring this up with the physician if the sample area was on a different floor from where you were meeting?
2. What would you do if the problem persisted and the physician or staff seemed unmotivated to help?

Red Flags:
1. Complaining or whining about the competitor to the physician is unacceptable.
2. Getting flustered or frustrated instead of planning how to deal with the situation creatively.

Q. How do you handle selling more than one product on the same call and set it apart from the competition? Let's say it's a new product approved by the FDA.

What they want to see:
Even seasoned pharmaceutical reps cringe when having to sell two products at once. This typically occurs when the FDA approves a new drug. The interviewer wants you to recognize this situation requires more sales strategy, product knowledge, and enhanced communication skills.

Answer:
"I believe launching a newly approved product would be exciting. And I'd be enthusiastic when introducing the product during office visits, dinners, and lunches with clients. Initially, I'd focus on clients who I have the best rapport with or those I've identified as cutting edge purchasers. The physicians who traditionally like to try new products.

I'd use the new product as a reason to call on prospects who previously turned me down or haven't bought my main pill. Selling two products can be tricky. It would require having a clear understanding of my audience so I knew which product to lead with.

Once I had a couple physician groups using my product, I could use them as testimonials or talking points with other prospects. If price ever became an issue, I would already have micro phrases prepared about how the product is more efficacious than the competition and its value to their patients would summon a positive ROI for the practice."

What this says about you:
1. You have a general idea and game plan how to sell two products simultaneously.
2. You handle change easier than most and are mentally adaptable to the business.

Follow up questions: *(Based on this answer)*
1. What would you do if the product began selling and was suddenly pulled off the market by the FDA?
2. What would you do if all your attempts at selling the new product failed?

Red Flags:
1. Anyone who says introducing a new product would be easy will lose credibility instantly in the interview.

2. Asking too many clarifying questions:

- "What type of new product is it?"
- "Is the price point close to my old product?"
- "Will it take the place of my old product?" is annoying.

The interviewer wants to see how you think not be interrogated.

Q. How would you go about getting more time with a doctor?

What they want to see:
If you were interviewing with me, I'd be looking for your level of creativity and drive in getting more face-to-face selling time with your clients.

Answer:
"My experience is, a happy staff makes for a happy executive. In this case, it would be a happy physician. I would find out what the office staff likes: Exotic teas, custom Sherpa pen cases, movie tickets, calendars, groupon vouchers, etc. I would then ask the staff what's the best way to get more one-on-one time with the physician(s). Typically, they'd tell me the best time of day to come in, where they like to golf, swim, have dinner, hike, and hang out.

I'd also follow the physician on any social media to see where they express interest and really listen to their comments.

I'd pay close attention to see if the physician likes to give back to the community: The Boys and Girls Clubs, a local little league baseball or basketball team, fundraisers, and galas. I'd align my approach based on where their heart lies. I have more ideas but that's a start. This is exactly why I keep a journal entry on every office. You never know when these notes come in handy 3 or 6 months later."

What this says about you:
1. You have creative ideas and have dealt with similar situations.

2. You think strategically (Social media, keeping a journal).

Follow up questions: *(Based on this answer)*
1. How would you overcome the stigma of your predecessor's poor attitude and customer service?
2. What would you do if the doctor made it clear he doesn't fraternize with reps outside of work?

Red Flags:
1. If you don't show some form of enthusiasm or if you're not being up to the challenge of building client relationships. Expect more follow up questions to gauge your worthiness for this position.

2. If your version of creativity is to bring donuts and coffee to every visit.

Q. Give me an example of one of your most challenging sales?

What they want to see:
This is a straightforward question. What's your definition of challenging? What's your approach to solving problems? Can you briefly articulate how you overcame a challenge to make the sale happen?

Answer:
Use the **S.T.A.R.** format for situational questions.

Situation:
"I remember having an appointment with a customer who experienced less than excellent customer service with a previous sales rep from our company. Dr. Charles wouldn't take my calls for a month, thinking I was the other rep.

Task:
I first had to convince him, through his staff, that I was a new rep and this would be a new experience; and that my attention to detail, product knowledge, and follow through could save him thousands on his bottom line.

Action:
It took 77 days to earn a second chance and get a face-to-face

appointment. After our initial meeting and letting him voice his frustrations, which were many, he accepted a limited number of samples. It took another two months and four additional visits before he added my product to his lineup. One day, a member of his staff pulled me to the side and said my dogged persistence and calm demeanor is what turned Dr. Charles around.

Result:
He signed the contract and wrote a letter to my boss. In fact, here you go." (Slide the rave review across the table to the interviewer.)

What this says about you:
1. You can speak about a bad situation and not point fingers or slander the previous rep.
2. You're persistent and have the ability to execute long-term goals (77 days).

Follow up questions: (Based on this answer)
1. How exactly did you convince Dr. Charles' staff to give you a chance?
2. Tell me the exact moment you believed you received the green light to close the sale?

Red Flags:
1. If you're example is simple or weak. It naturally makes you look like a lessor candidate when others provide stronger examples. Use your toughest or most interesting sales experience here.

2. Being long winded with your answer only demonstrates how equally long winded you'd be in front of an intolerant physician and not a good fit for pharm sales.

BONUS:

Would you prefer to select a new dentist based on a commercial advertisement or utilize the recommendation of a well respected friend? Correct, from a friend.

Understand and use the power of testimonials.

Attach several testimonial documents to your application package. During the interview, modestly share micro conversations of what clients and superiors say about your performance, skill sets, character, and 'IT' factor.

Q. What strengths do you bring to this position?

What they want to see:

When the district or regional manger stares you straight in the eyes and asks you this question; they want to see, hear, and feel a connection to your answer. Are you confident enough? Are you over-confident? Do you say you have good communication skills but mumble your words in the interview? Do they see career congruency in you? Specifically, does what you say about yourself match up with the skills needed to be a Rockstar pharm sales rep?

Answer:

"I read in a book once, "listening for deep listening." I listen to what people say past their words. Like your question about my strengths, I'm thinking you want to know if I really have the personality and skills to do this job or if I'm all fluff? I believe interactive listening helps you connect with people quickly and easily.

Speaking of connecting, my boss and my friends keep telling me I have that 'IT' factor when it comes to connecting with people.

A mentor taught me you can teach someone a skill but you can't teach an attitude. It's the factor that affects your persistence, productivity, results, and more. No wheelchair, no eye patch, no chemo is what I say each morning for an attitude gratitude check.

Finally, I'm hungry...hungry to learn, master, teach, and learn again. I believe when you listen, check your attitude daily, and are hungry to master a new skill, all you need is a vehicle like this career and even the sky has no limits."

What this says about you:

1. You're different than other candidates because your answer is different, it's original, it's you.
2. You're trainable. Here you are speaking about what a mentor taught you, reciting a phrase from a book.

Follow up questions: (Based on this answer)

1. Tell me exactly how you'd use one of those strengths to call on an old lead?
2. Those are nice soft skills, what hard skills do you possess?

Red Flags:
1. Listing more than 5 strengths in one question isn't wise. Research shows adult memory significantly fades when remembering 7 or more items at once.
2. If you're not akin to talking nice about yourself in public...practice, practice, practice. Your tone and enthusiasm must match your description or you'll seem emotionally fraudulent.

Wrap it up:

1. University You

I've seen candidates research an organization they're interviewing with to perfection, but when it came to researching their internal inventory: skills, likes, dislikes, strengths, and value driven points…they fell short. And so too did the job offer. Study 'You' first!

2. Everybody's in Sales

I love hearing a new RYI student say, *"But I'm not in sales."* I smile silently and say, *"You haven't sold me on the fact that you're not in sales."* If you don't learn to sell yourself in the interview, who will?

3. Personality vs. Commodity

If your resume, college pedigree, skills, and training are the same as the other finalist, how do employers select the winner? By personality, the intangibles, or the "IT" factor. The candidate that gives original answers laced with value driven experience will win every day that ends in "Y" (Minus the standard getting juiced into a position due to relationships).

4. Relationships 101

Any executive worth her weight in gold will tell you, it's all about building Teflon relationships. It's not who you know, but who you know that will 'take action' on your behalf, at your request, or through your influence.

Women Only:
Learn skills to succeed in any highly competitive environment:

Get Instant Access:
www.rockstaryourinterview.com

15

Closing the deal

Asking for the job

I rarely say the word never; however, it's in the dictionary for a reason. When you make it this far in the interview process, become incredibly relaxed and overconfident only if you want to watch your opportunity float away like a dandelion seed riding a strong breeze.

"The interview is never over!"

Einstein said, "*Energy cannot be created or destroyed, it can only be changed from one form to another.*" Treat the interview with the same respect. The energy of the interview merely changes forms.

In each phase of earning a position you're continuously being interviewed formally and informally. Similar to a relationship leading up to marriage or cohabiting together, the interview is to merely establish you're not dating a serial killer. That's only the first date. The interview relationship is a continuous process that changes from one form to another. During your entire interview process act accordingly.

Q. Is there anything else you would like to add to help us make a decision?

What they want to hear:
Sell. Sell. Sell. This is an invitation for you to review, literally ask for the position, and reiterate your value.

Answer:
"*Yes Tina, there is. Correct me if I'm wrong, but during our conversation you said getting more foot traffic in all 5 locations is priority number one? And that traditional marketing methods are trending downward?*

Well, my last three years have been specifically geared toward aligning web-based marketing life cycles with traditional profiles. By adding unique online campaigns and modestly repositioning your brand, I estimate foot traffic will increase by 23% and customer engagement will rise from your current 27% to at least 43%.

See, I base my projections on research I conducted using your company's own marketing analysis. If you can't tell by now, solving problems is exciting to me. I'm a techy with a personality. That's why I created a market think tank comprised of 54 other professionals dedicated to solving problems, growing revenue, and creating unique emotional experiences for customers, not just sales. Do you have a laptop we can use so I can show you a couple of examples?"

What this says about you:
1. You've been an effective listener during the interview.
2. You have a sense of humor and can poke fun at yourself.
3. You understand statistics, ratios, and monetary impact.

Follow up Questions: *(based on this answer)*
1. How did you get involved with your 'think tanks'?
2. Where did you get your statistical data?

Red Flags:
1. Not asking for the job.
2. Losing focus, low enthusiasm, or not able to convey your value.

Q. Your recruiter told me the salary you're looking for. I'm curious as it seems low, considering your background and experience?

What they want to hear:

That money isn't the issue now and won't be for the next 18 months. They want to see and believe that you're not taking the salary because you're desperate, getting by until a larger offer arrives, and/or that they're not wasting their time.

Answer:

"Larry, I know you picked up on the fact that my salary hasn't changed in the last two years. That's because our organization has been on a salary freeze and implanted mandatory furloughs to cut costs rather than employ layoffs. Thank you for noticing my experience. With the extra time, I invested in skills workshops, the new matrix software, and volunteered at Proxy Labs to be exposed to thought leading philosophies.

In fact, volunteering is how I came across your organization. Someone mentioned it during conversation, I researched and was surprised to discover my skills naturally align with your mission of forward thinking and cutting edge product development. And your culture is kin to promote from within.

Look Larry, I'm willing to pay my dues and bring more value to the table than my proposed salary. To be on a team where I'm excited to come to work every day...is number one, the money will take care of itself."

What this says about you:
1. You addressed a potential conflict question directly and succinctly.
2. You didn't blame your current organization for unexpected happenings.
3. You're not a victim. You're a fighter, action taker, and problem solver.

Follow up Questions: *(based on this answer)*
1. How did that make you feel when your career plans began to crumble?
2. What if the money doesn't take care of itself in the first two years?

Red Flags:
1. If you make money an issue in any way during future conversations leading up to the offer.
2. If you're not able to answer the follow up questions with the same tact and fervor as the initial question.

Q. You come from a small, tight knit, highly dysfunctional company. I know because I used to work there. We're the same here: small, tight knit, and highly dysfunctional. Your quality of life won't change, the salary and benefits aren't amazingly different, why do you want to leave to come here?

What do they want to see:

Can you say final test? With this question the interviewer is waiting for you to shine or flat line. It's your job to highlight what you believe is different about the companies.

Answer:

"Great, it sounds like I'm a perfect fit (big smile when you say this). But seriously. Gary, although two puzzles may look like the same picture, the pieces that make up the picture are typically unique. Even though the cultures are similar I see your company completely different. I researched your clients, the talent you've recruited, and your revenue statistics.

You play in a higher end market. 72% of your revenue comes from 23% of your clients. You like to recruit from Cornell University and their school is notorious for influencing our industry with technology and online revenue sources. I have a few ideas of my own how to diversify the risk of a down turning market to make a portfolio recession proof.

Working here, I'd be in my power swing, dealing with higher end clients, similar forward thinking co-workers, and a part of a higher standard of service. These are all 'to be mastered' skills included in my personal goals for this year. And to be direct, Gary, I'm looking forward to working with you. More times than I can count, I've listened to people say, "It'd be different if Gary were here." You left a reputation as a savant problem solver, a visionary, and just a great human being to work for. That's why I'm proposing to bring my value to your team."

What this says about you:

1. You did your mega-research, and demonstrated you have value and

ideas.

2. You have personal goals and demonstrate personal accountability.

3. You can give structured compliment without the appearance of being a kiss-ass.

Follow up Questions: *(based on this answer)*

1. What makes you think you're qualified to play in this 'high end' market?

2. Where did you get your statistical data?

Red Flags:

1. If you do not provide specific details with respect to why you want to leave.

2. If you are unable to provide evidence of the value you hold.

Q. Is there anything else about you I should know?

What they want to see:

I've seen a six-figure job disappear like a shadow in sunlight because she chose not to disclose having a domestic dispute arrest in her background. And it was a true case of self-defense, nothing to be ashamed of. When you receive a verbal job offer and a question similar to this one follows, now is the time to lay all your cards on the table. If the organization can't accept you and your past, do you really want to be there anyway?

Of course, if your background is cleaner than Appalachian wild spring water at 13,000 ft., you can answer with something interesting about yourself or quickly move to closing the deal. Let's review an answer with a past.

Answer:

"Yes James,...there is. 11 years ago on March 21st, I made a stupid decision. I drove while intoxicated and received a DUI. No one was hurt expect my pride. I accept full responsibility for my actions and offer zero excuses for my poor judgment that night.

Since then, I've spoken more than 13 times to high school and college students about how DUI's follow you for life and encouraged them to use the many resources, available now days, to get rides instead of getting behind the wheel. To date, my driving record is clean. I hope a few bad hours of my life won't over shadow the recent 10 years of peak performance or dissuade you from considering me for this position."

What this says about you:
1. You accept responsibility.
2. You turned a mess into success (DUI speaker/advocate).

Follow up Questions: *(based on this answer)*
1. Are you positive that's the only thing I need to know about?
2. Outside of the obvious, not breaking the law, what major lesson did you take from the situation?

Red Flags:
1. Lying or stretching the truth about facts in your checkered past.
2. Not disclosing anything that will blindside your new employer: Military commitments, out of country vacations, or similar personal engagements.

"Certainty + Commitment + Drive = Sexy"

Q. If you were offered the job when could you start?

What they want to see:
If your soon to be husband was cheating on his current wife, would you trust him completely? The interviewer wants to see genuine respect for your current employer and a time frame that's appropriate for your position and industry. For most, two weeks is commonplace. For executives with quarterly profit irons in the fire: One, two, or even three months may be appropriate.

Answer:
"Currently, I have an important project on the table. I must see it through so my team makes their goal. So, three weeks."

What this says about you:
1. You think about the effect on others.
2. You finish what you start.

Follow up Questions: *(based on this answer)*
1. Is there anyway we can get you on board sooner?
2. This position travels 30% of the time, how do you feel about that?

Red Flags:
1. If you give a large window of time, *"say...two to four weeks"*. Be as specific as possible. Provide a brief reason if your request to start is more than two weeks. Remember, they've probably been understaffed for a hot minute and are itching to get someone on board.

2. If you don't ask for enough time up front. Extending your initial agreement of two weeks to three weeks, without a valid emergency reason, casts doubt in your new employer's mind. They may think this about you:

- *"Is he still interviewing?"*
- *"Is she holding out for another offer?"*
- *"Is he staying at his current company?"* And so on.

BONUS:

Whether before, during, or after the interview...squeeze in the fact that you are always willing to teach co-workers or share what you know to make their job easier.

Don't say the word Teamwork...demonstrate it.

Q. Are you considering other job offers right now?

What do they want to see:
Riddle me this, can you think of one reason saying 'yes' would benefit the company you're interviewing with? While there are exceptions to every rule, in general, it's best to let this company know that 'at that moment' you're not entertaining other job offers. Would you be more or less attracted to a man who said he was choosing between you and one of your girlfriends to be his woman? Need I say more?

Answer:
"Janet, I researched and selected this position because this is where I want to be. No other companies have my attention right now."

What this says about you:
1. You're committed and want the position.
2. You are less of a risk if offered the position.

Follow up Questions: *(based on this answer)*
None.

Red Flags:
1. Trying to look important or in demand by stating you have multiple offers.
2. Using this question as a chance to brazenly barter for a higher salary. Yes, there are exceptions and executive positions are different. The 'art of negotiation' is a book all by itself.

Q. What salary would be fair for both of us?

What do they want to see:
Well, isn't this a delicious piece of $500.00 cheese placed neatly on the rattrap? Do not fall for it. This is a beautiful example of a passive aggressive tactic to entice you to toss out a number first.

The experienced interviewer wants to see how you think when negotiating. Utilize this question as a tool to dig up highlights during the interview and ask what value the interviewer would place on a candidate with such skills.

Answer:
"Cindy, I could give you a straight answer if I knew what skills you believe are most valuable for this position. My power-swing skills are relationship development, sophisticated problem solving, and technical expertise. Hopefully, I've illustrated that throughout the interview. I'm sure you at least have a range in mind?"

What this says about you:
1. You can operate in a negotiation conversation with tact (and are displaying your power swing skill of relationship development).
2. This isn't your first negotiation rodeo.

Follow up Questions: *(based on this answer)*
1. I appreciate your tact. Please answer the question?
2. Okay, I'll lead. $94k - $143k. What's your number?

Red Flags:
1. Refusing to answer directly when prompted.
2. If you start with an outlandish and unfair salary, be prepared to back peddle and rebuild the trust you just lost.

NOTE: If you sense the interviewer is a no nonsense woman and she presses you to answer, give her what she wants. Begin on the mid to medium-high end for negotiating room. If you did your research, you'll already have a credible range for this position in mind.

Wrap this Burrito up

1. Fresh Mental Produce
As soon as you exit the interview. Write down at least three things you did well and three things you could improve on. It's best while fresh. Did any questions throw you off? Was your research up to par? How effective was your interview body language?

2. K.I.T.
Keep in touch. Send a hand written thank you letter or email to the interviewer(s) ASAP. I prefer hand written letters because they're tangible, visible, and 90% of candidates don't do it.

Be a personality not a commodity.

3. Journal
Scribe the names and details of the experience: When you walked in, culture, secretary's name, interviewer likes/dislikes, and other candidates you ran into. You never know whom you'll cross paths with in the future. Believe this, keeping an interview journal can earn you a job.

4. Modify
Was anything unclear to your interviewer? Do you need to make modifications to your resume, interview cheat notes, testimonials, or references?

5. Reward
Congratulate yourself and celebrate. My tradition after an interview would be to visit Marshalls, T.J Max, or Ross and buy a plush new wardrobe of socks. Don't laugh too hard. I know I'm weird...and I like it.

16

Your Turn

After the interview is over questions

Asking strategic, concise, and well-crafted questions with enthusiasm makes your interviewer think, "*Oh, she really is interested in this position.*" Your questions have the ability to:

✓ Build additional rapport with your interviewer(s).
✓ Summarize key points from your conversation.
✓ Demonstrate your preparation, research, and underscore your value.
✓ Recall an important emotional point that occurred during the conversation.

Leading off your question with a micro introduction, that reminds the interviewer of a stand-out moment, will separate you from the competition. For example:

> "*Ms. James, earlier you mentioned technology playing a big role in product development. What version of software and equipment will this position be working with?*"

> "*Ken, hopefully my experience at Mircofirm shows I can surpass sales goals in a recession climate, how would you describe the culture of your team?*"

Take a few moments to review the sets of questions below. Which ones feel and appear to be the most natural for you to ask?

Questions About the Organization:

- What's your overall hiring philosophy?
- What's been your most memorable experience here?
- What's the percentage of part time vs. full time employees?
- Do you foresee any acquisitions in the near future?
- What's your market share of the industry?
- What are the company's top 2 priorities in the next 2 years?
- What are your most profitable distribution channels?
- Does your company use more online marketing campaigns or online advertising?
- How has technology impacted your workflow?
- What innovations have your customers insisted on in the last 6-18 months?
- What does your supply chain look like from raw material to a customer's hands? (***Careful:*** *you don't want your interviewer to*

fear you may be after his job. Use a humble or inquisitive tone.)

Questions About the Team:

- Can you describe the org chart for the department?
- What outside departments would be interacted with the most?
- What are the top 2 priorities of the department in the next 2 years?
- On a scale of 1-10, how well is creativity accepted in this department? For this position?
- What's the number 1 problem the department is facing?
- How would you describe the culture of the department?
- How many direct reports does this position have? Do any have direct reports of their own?

Questions About the Position:

- What functions in the job description make up 80% of a typical day?
- Are there major roles not listed on the job description?
- How did this position become available?
- How long has this position been vacant?
- What's the environment like around the work area?
- What versions of software and hardware are being used?
- What qualities should a candidate have to be successful in this position?

Questions About Moving Forward:

- Who will I be interviewing with next?
- Can you tell me a little about the next person I'll be interviewing with?
- When would be your ideal day to fill this position?
- What does your timeline look like to make a decision?

Five Types of Questions not to Ask:

Questions that:

1. Reveal your bias -*"Does everyone speak good English here?"*

2. Make the interviewer uncomfortable – *"Are you married? Are you a mixed race?"*
3. Jokes of any kind. No example necessary.
4. Arrogantly assume the position – *"What's your first goal for my team?"*
5. Show your ignorance – *"What's the core business of the company?"*

Asking strategic, concise, and well-crafted questions, with a hint of practical psychology, helps round out the interviewer's willingness to select you over other candidates. Listen for the style of your interviewer and formulate your questions accordingly.

For example, if the interviewer is technically oriented, use numbers and statistics to illustrate your value. If the interviewer is highly descriptive and creative by nature, use pictures and analogies to illuminate your self-worth.

Above all,

"be genuinely interested"

in the answer when you ask questions. Everyone has a BS meter and it behooves you to lack genuine enthusiasm and curiosity...because it will show.

It's paramount you work on your individual skills first, then bring your brilliance to the Team. Value begins with you.

17

After the Interview

What's next?

Once you shake hands with your interviewer and step off the Rock Star Stage, you'll probably want to get the heck of dodge and let your hair down.

Just remember, the interview is never over. You have just planted a relationship seed that may show up 7 weeks, 7 months, or 7 years down the road in your career path. Therefore, water the new relationship with care.

Write a thank you note to all your interviewers. Keep it short and sweet. Say thank you and mention one or two memorable points about the interview.

I'm often asked, "*How do I know what's memorable*?" Well, what did your interviewer show you? Think about:

- ✓ When your interviewer laughed
- ✓ When they told you a story
- ✓ Drilled down on a specific topic
- ✓ What they were wearing
- ✓ When they frowned

All these 'tell signs' give you clues about what to say in your thank you note. Just like the interview you want the thank you letter to be memorable and unique. You can take the risk and sound like everyone else, outlining your strengths and trying to sell, sell, sell, yourself once more. Or you can Go Opposite and speak to your interviewer's emotional I.Q..

Of course, you should mention one or two of your qualities that are of value to the organization. Again, take the interviewer's lead. What did they show you that was valuable from their perspective? What interests did they convey during your conversation? Take those prized pieces of information and infuse them into your thank you note.

For Example:

Hi Jenny,

A humble thank you for granting me an interview for the Regional Manager position. Your openness and genuine personality made me feel at home. I appreciate your compliment on my teamwork skills and how I handled the ironing board situation.

Next time you visit family back home in Albuquerque, have one of those Christmas burritos for me too.

Make it a great day,

Paul

Paul 'tall guy, pink tie' Anderson

The keys to a great thank you letter are:

- ✓ be brief,
- ✓ be memorable
- ✓ be specific

Write a nine-paragraph, full page Sunday morning editorial response only *if you don't want the job.* What busy manager has time to read long-winded thank you responses? Think. Time is an ultra-precious resource to busy decision makers.

Which Method?
The avenue of delivery you use for the thank you card depends mainly on the interviewer's style. Did they give you any clues such as, "*I hardly ever have time to check email,*" "*I'm old fashioned,*" or did they use words like, "*time-honored?*"

Again, the clues they leave behind determines what delivery method to use when sending a thank you note.

When in doubt, do both. Write a quick thank you email directly after the interview (like the prior example) and send a hand written note with information that's helpful to the interviewer.

For Example:

"Hi Jane, during the interview I remember you saying you were looking for a good guitar instructor for your son. Here are two great teachers. They'll also be solid leads for other instructors, in the event their teaching style doesn't match with your son's learning style. Gotta Run."

Jamie Kerrigan

"Hi James, I came across this article on trending sales ratios at my leadership group. You mentioned it during our conversation as a challenge for a couple of managers. I highlighted the major points to save you time. Stay focused! And Happy Memorial Day to you and your family."

Ricky "Red Socks" Sanchez

"Be brief, be memorable, and be specific."

18

~Energy~

Hybrid Fuel – Power your interview

Have you ever heard of the 'IT' factor? With respect to interviewing, it's the candidate who leaves the interviewers in the room feeling inspired, impressed, and remembering the quality of their answers. What exactly makes a person change the way an interviewer feels? How can some candidates, for the most part, provide similar answers as others, yet their delivery appears to set them apart from the competition? Can you relate to this? The answer is...

Energy = Enthusiasm

I'm sure you instinctively know this; however, when's the last time you practiced generating energy specifically for interview purposes? 7 out of 10 interviewers are unable to explain how they are able to generate or modulate their energy prior to stepping in the room, much less when they're in the moment. Here are four common but less than commonly used ways to generate energy:

1. Food
2. Actions
3. Supplements
4. Thoughts

DISCLAIMER: Please consult your doctor before trying any suggestions mentioned in this text. The information is provided for experimentation purposes only. Each person's body is an individual ecology.

FOOD:

Your body is the car, food is the fuel. If you and I both eat the same size banana from the same bunch, our bodies will produce different amounts of energy. That's because each body is unique. Your small intestines are a different size than mine. They absorb the nutrients and digested food at a different rate than mine. So what does that mean?

The first nutritional expert you should trust is you. If you want to deliver a higher performing interview, understand how your body processes proteins, carbohydrates, sugars, and cruciferous vegetables.

"Experiment with food and your body."

5 Brilliant Brain foods:

- Walnuts
- Broccoli
- Chocolate (Raw/unprocessed)
- Avocado
- Spinach

Create your own supercharged superfood RYI smoothies @
www.RockStarYourInterview.com

ACTIONS:

Increased blood circulation = more oxygen to the brain = more energy for the power plant = faster processing speed = potentially higher quality answers.

1. The day of the interview, wake up to a fast paced morning walk, light workout, or yoga routine

2. The week of the interview; exercise until you sweat, then immediately after, review your interview strategy. (while a large amount of oxygen is circulating through the brain)

3. Before entering the building or the room: In the bathroom, do 5 slow and easy standing squats. Only go half way down if you're in a skirt and heels. Do not attempt this if you have any physical injuries.

4. Breathing patterns: Before entering the environment. Close your eyes, imagine your breath taking the shape of translucent bright blue smoke. Each breath passes in and out through your heart. 23 seconds is plenty. Take more time if your stress level dictates.

5. Strike a power pose in any mirror or reflective surface 10 minutes prior

to interviewing.

Google "Amy Cuddy – *Power Poses*" for an entertaining way to use the actions of your body to harness energy and power for your interview.

SUPPLEMENTS:

Nootropics, a term made popular by Romanian chemist Dr. Giurgea, are chemicals/supplements/foods that have scientific evidence of boosting brainpower.

Google the word, "Nootropics," poke around and see what catches your attention. This area of thinking is as polarized as a dirty martini, you either like it or you don't.

When looking at the brain and its relationship to your memories, you have to consider several factors which increase the ability to store, process, and recall information:

1. Increased blood flow
2. Cellular regeneration and communication (fire and wiring)
3. Reduced inflammation

5 Nootropic Powerhouse Protocols

1. Piracetam

A chemical drug that excites neuron activity in the brain. Praised by the North American and European CEO community.

2. Artichoke Extract and Forskolin (stacked/taken together)
   A natural food extract that produces a calm acute alertness and magnified memory skills.

3. Acetyl-L-Carnitine (ALCAR)
   Promotes the production of memory chemicals and enhanced brain functions.

4. Resveratrol

Considered an anti-aging agent. Naturally found in grapes. Helps with cellular regenerative functions.

5. Ginkgo biloba

A strong anti-oxidant and natural tree product that advocates cellular healing and regeneration functions.

"Some of the most important conversations are the ones you have with yourself."

THOUGHTS:

Every thought creates a chemical reaction in your body.

Holster that thought for a moment. Forget scientific theory, double blind studies with placebo factors, data integrity, and all that bullship (I call it bullship to grab your unconscious attention). It's just you and me talking right now. Let's say you rose to begin your day at 5:00 A.M., it ended at 11:00 P.M., you're exhausted, and pass out on the bed with your clothes on.

The phone rings at 2:00 A.M., someone you love is in the hospital, scared, and pleading for your help. Are you exhausted anymore? Of course not, thoughts involving the situation have summoned energy reserves.

This is the power of thoughts, the power to change your body chemistry in seconds. Thoughts are dual directional. The example above is based on reaction, fear, and emergency. Let's walk the other direction with a proactive intent. How can we use thought to enhance the performance of your future interviews?

Imagine yourself laughing as you walk out the door and a bright, lagoon blue light disappearing as it closes behind you. Speak in the past tense and say with a smile, "It felt amazing to receive the job offer that fast" or something similar.

The key to manufactured thoughts creating lasting changes to your biochemistry is the ability to get the goose bumps by creating pictures in the your mind.

All these methods: Food, Actions, Supplements, and Thoughts, used separately, have a positive impact on your 'IT' factor. When used in conjunction with one another, your probability of Rock Starring your interview increases radically.

Rock Star Your Interview Inspiration

The Return of Destiny

A day of reflection energies transpired, an objective look at our results vs desires...

As we lay here in silence rustles from leaves, Allow thoughts to flow in and out with ease...

Is success that simple like a dandelion seed, effortlessly riding the kiss of a breeze...

I yearn to remember this is what I expect, reverse actions of what it means to forget…

With memory's return and fears laid in check,

Today..

Toward my destiny I will take one step...

Your interview is a rhythmic poetry waiting to happen.

London

Creative Exercise 1
Product Intelligence

Recently, I was taking a tour through Ocean Spray's plant in Henderson, NV, on the outskirts of Las Vegas. The technology manager was providing statistics about the corporation. It was interesting to know that more than 25% of Ocean Spray's annual sales were derived from supplying Walmart's global gorilla distribution.

In the spirit of Walmart-conversation, the technology manager stopped at the end of the assembly line where the bottles were ready to be capped, boxed, loaded, and shipped to market. My host explained how Walmart suggested and incorporated the installation of an electronic device that reads the quantity of bottles produced before they leave the assembly line. I had an ah-hah moment. Walmart intrigued me with their attention to detail concerning certainty.

Pause: Allow your creative juices to breathe in the possibilities of what Walmart could leverage this data for...

At any given time, Walmart could be 'certain' of how many bottles of product were available to sell, without having to research Ocean Spray's supply capacity. (Assuming there is a known percentage of the plants total production dedicated to Walmart.) Do you see how this product intelligence accelerates the effect of technology on globalization?

"Once you make a decision, the universe conspires to make it happen."

Back to the story. When it's 7:00am in Las Vegas, what time is it in Beijing, China? Correct, 2:00 am (they are in the future 2:00 am). Imagine this, a global sales executive for Walmart strikes a deal with a

Beijing supplier to increase their export potential by 50.5 million US dollars annually; wouldn't it be nice if the executive could extrapolate real time data from the supplier (Ocean Spray) to verify the supply-chain could meet the demand of the deal? Absolutely. How long would it take the sales exec to locate the same data if this device wasn't in place?

Furthermore, why did Ocean Spray allow Walmart to have such intimate electronic access to their distribution plants? Answer, if 25% of your current salary came from your mother-in-law, would you allow her to put a GPS device on your car to detect where you were at all times? She's paying 25% of the car-note. Well, maybe that wasn't the best example, but it's funny to me and you get the point.

Your homework:

1. Look around your work environment or at home.
2. Think Product Intelligence (PI).
3. How can PI improve one function you do regularly?

This is a mental exercise. Whether you're selling computer chips or cow chips, work in private sector or public sector, if you're a university librarian or work at the Library of Congress...how can you incorporate a mirco-story of product intelligence to **Rock Star Your** next **Interview**?

Creative Exercise 2
It Doesn't Count

During your interview journey there will be moments when you feel frustrated, tired, unworthy, and experience moments of self-doubt. It happens to us all. Conventional wisdom would tell you to shake it off, don't listen, or put up a good fight. **Screw that.**

Go Opposite. Invite all those negative emotions to run wild and play freely in your cranium because they're already there. Just put a time clock on em'. Allow yourself to feel whatever that negative feeling is, but only for 5 minutes, 10 minutes, but no longer than 15. And when the alarm sounds, the negativity has to go play somewhere else. Deal? Put a clock on it.

When bad thoughts attempt to return, because they will, say out loud,

"IT DOESN'T COUNT!"

When you're too physically and emotionally tired to defend yourself against yourself; remember, it doesn't count. Any bad thought you can think of:

- 23 resumes sent, no response
- 7 interviews, no offer
- They didn't call because I'm too short
- too bald, too fat, too black
- too butch, I'm not smart enough, I can't do this
- I should quit dreaming, quit looking, quit trying
- I should just quit

SMILE and say firmly
"IT DOESN'T COUNT!"

Only address self-doubt when you're in a strong mental, physical, and emotional state. Only when you can view those thoughts objectively.

Creative Exercise 3
Sex is Important

Pardon my exclusivity Ladies; however, this exercise is for guys only. Please don't read this page. Gentleman, being an author, I get to rub elbows with other authors. A friend of mine, Maddy Dychtwald wrote:

INFLUENCE: *How Women's Soaring Economic Power Will Transform Our World for the Better.*

On page 83 and 84, she speaks about women making, "*83% of consumer purchases in the United States.*"

And...

- ✓ 62% of new cars
- ✓ 92% of vacations
- ✓ 90% of food
- ✓ 94% of home furnishing

Inside the book, she cites how women live longer than men and, mathematically speaking, it's only a matter of time before women have the financial pendulum swinging in their direction. If you're going to succeed in business long term, allow the research and findings in INFLUENCE to be a resource on your journey.

So, the question I have is, what are you doing to understand a woman's motivation? How will such knowledge help you build instant rapport when you interview with a woman, a panel of women, or interview in a feminine industry? What about when you have a conversation with a stranger (who is a woman) at Whole Foods, in a club, or standing in line at the bank?

C'mon, man! I'm not asking you to be metrosexual, I'm inviting you to be a critical thinker about how to improve your conversation with women in your interviews and in your everyday life. **Don't change who you are,**

change what you know.

Your homework:

1. Watch the first 33 minutes of: **The Devil Wears Prada**
Think about this one centering thought during the movie. What motivates a woman? And how can you place your skills in the pathway of her motivation?

2. Check out the book: **Women Come First**, By: Ian Kerner, Ph.D. Read pages 29-31. For the eBook version, read the first four pages of Chapter 5.

3. Pop in your local library and pick up Maddy's book INFLUENCE or download it now from Amazon. Begin to ask questions and understand how your current position or your business is and can be influenced by the growing discretionary income and wealth of women.

MEN – MONEY - SEX

When Steve Jobs transitioned over to the other side, who inherited his economic influence?...Mrs. Jobs.

When Bill Gates transitions, who will inherit his economic influence?...Melinda.

Warren Buffet? Mrs. Buffet.
Do you see where I'm going with this?

THINK! THINK! THINK!

Creative Exercise 4
Emotional Intelligence in Action

A great way to develop emotional intelligence and mental toughness skills simultaneously is through action. Intentionally put yourself in a 'trigger based' situation and around points of view you commonly disagree with. For example:

If you lean toward a conservative, Republican mode of thinking:

- Watch a segment of the Ed Schultz Show
- Listen to 10 minutes of Don Imus' radio show
- Find one issue to compliment the Democratic party on

If you lean toward a liberal, Democratic style of thinking:

- Watch a segment of the Bill O'Reilly Show
- Listen to 10 minutes of the Rush Limbaugh radio show
- Find one issue to compliment the Republican party on

If you could care less about anything political.

- Watch a segment of any political TV Show
- Listen to 10 minutes of any political Radio Show.
- Find one reason to compliment politics in general

Watch your emotions like a hawk. See what words, thoughts, and actions get the best of you or make you upset without your permission. Do you want to put yourself to the test now or when you're in a live interview?

Creative Exercise 5
Merge and Purge Fridays

When is the last time you cleaned out:

- That kitchen drawer with everything in it?
- Your garage?
- Your clothes closet?
- Your car or truck's middle console?
- The inside of your refrigerator?

How many times a year do you clean out your mental 'crap'? Do you believe it's possible that too many negative thoughts can suffocate brilliant ones?

ENTER: Merge and Purge Fridays

Disclaimer: This exercise is a tool not a rule. Modify at will. First, choose the day that works best for you. Friday's are functional for me. Every Friday evening, I take 3-7 minutes to forgive all the negative comments I received and delivered. I make it a point to separate the words away from who I am as a human being.

I understand the roles I play as a father, lover, giver, intellectual, friend, co-worker, black man, gentleman, rouge, athlete, and more. All those labels don't represent who I am; they're only roles I play. Therefore, I cleanse myself of the week's mental bull-ship to start the next week anew.

Every week, my mantra is different but here's part of a recent example I recorded:

> *Today, I'm merging and purging anything that doesn't serve me. I am grateful. I am blessed. I have God within. This week I forgive:*
>
> *• Jokingly being called a dumbass for the mistake I made on an important report.*

- *Myself for not paying attention to my son when he was telling me about his class project.*
- *The white woman for calling me a nigger after confusing me with another man who stole her parking space.*
- *Myself for not treating my body good by skipping two workouts.*
- *Myself for feeling fat because I ate the whole damn bucket of mint chocolate chip ice cream…by myself.*
- *My intellect for not researching Dr. Huggins research to verify its accuracy.*

All of these things have nothing to do with me and who I am. That's why I'm putting them in this mental trash bag, which I now throw away forever.

Amen

Rockstar Resource 1
RYI Checklist

Do Bring:

✓ A copy of your resume with notes for you to use during the interview

✓ Additional clean, quality copies of your resume (one per interviewer)

✓ Directions to the interview location (hard copy)

✓ Cell phone charger and your planning calendar

✓ A pen and medium sized notebook

✓ List of questions to ask about the position, department, and company

✓ Past work samples or your "portfolio" (if applicable)

✓ Name, title, department, and **phone #** of your interviewer or staff

✓ Breath mints, comb, or brush (don't ask, just do it)

✓ Compact mirror or smart phone with camera (hair, make up, face check)

✓ Cash (parking, toll, coffee, water, etc.)

✓ Your identification and Social Security Card
(for **when you Rock Star** your interview and get hired on the spot)

✓ An umbrella (even summer in Vegas or Phoenix, you never know)

Don't Bring

❖ Your cell phone inside OR turn it off

❖ A pants pocket full of stuff. Bulging pockets and jingling keys ain't sexy

❖ Your mom, dad, friends, or favorite pet

❖ No lattes, food, or gum chewing, please. A water bottle is okay

❖ **A bad attitude**

Rockstar Resource 2
RYI Cheat Sheet

Job Description Review

1. Position's Purpose
2. Position Success Factors

Your Micro-Stories (at least two of each)

- Micro-Story on Leadership
- Micro-Story on Teamwork, Conflict Resolution
- Micro-Story on Diversity, Mental Toughness
- Micro-Story on Specific Job Skill
- Micro-Story on Emotional Intelligence
- Micro-Story on Customer Service
- Micro-Story on Character and Trust

What Concrete Value Do You Bring To The Position

(Three key strengths and value points, based on your background)

1. _____

2. _____

3. _____

Organizational Research

Founded/Founders - Mission, Values, Culture - Industry Trends/Competitors - Fraternal Familial, or Professional Relationships - News Posting, Financial Statements, etc.

Social Medial: Linked In, RSS Feeds, Facebook, Twitter, Pinterest, etc.

Two Self-Improvement Traits

1. _____

2. _____

Know the Most Recent And Relevant Book You've Read

Rockstar Resource 3
Action Words for your Interview and Resume

1. Did you begin a task?

Activated	Formed	Initiated	Opened	Adopted
Founded	Instituted	Originated	Began	Generated
Introduced	Started	Established	Implemented	Launched

2. Did you think of something new?

Conceived	Devised	Invented	Solved	Discovered
Originated	Synergized	Created	Generated	Perceived
Synthesized	Designed	Improvised	Pioneered	Visualized
Developed	Innovated	Shaped	Conceptualized	

3. Did you provide something?

Dispensed	Installed	Presented	Responded	Distributed
Offered	Provided	Submitted	Fitted	Performed
Rendered	Supplied	Furnished		

4. Did you create something?

Assembled	Drew	Made	Programmed	Built
Engineered	Painted	Published	Composed	Fabricated
Photographed	Sketched	Constructed	Fashioned	Prepared
Drafted	Formed	Produced	Worked	Used

5. Did you acquire something new?

Acquired	Expanded	Purchased	Secured	Bought
Obtained	Raised	Solicited	Collected	Procured
Realized	Cultivated	Produced	Received	

6. Did you develop something?

Advanced	Enlarged	Increased	Surpassed	Augmented
Enriched	Modernized	Streamlined	Corrected	Expedited
Reduced	Treated	Cultivated	Extended	Resolved
Updated	Developed	Implemented	Revitalized	Upgraded
Enhanced	Improved	Solved		

7. How did you make changes?

Adapted	Extended	Refined	Standardized	Adopted
Extracted	Reorganized	Supplemented	Centralized	Implemented
Restored	Systematized	Combined	Improvised	Restructured
Synergized	Condensed	Modified	Revised	Tailored
Converted	Reconstructed	Separated	Unified	Edited
Redesigned	Simplified	United	Expanded	

8. What did you discover?

Ascertained	Discovered	Perceived	Solved	Determined
Found	Pinpointed	Uncovered	Detected	Identified
Proved	Verified	Diagnosed	Learned	Recognized

9. When were you the day's hero?

Averted	Prevented	Saved	Succeeded	Diverted
Salvaged	Withstood	Solved	Prevailed	

10. Did you cross the finish-line?

Achieved	Concluded	Finalized	Reached	Accomplished
Ended	Finished	Realized	Attained	Established
Fulfilled	Terminated	Completed	Executed	

11. What did you evaluate?

Analyzed	Compared	Perceived	Rated	Appraised
Evaluated	Qualified	Reasoned	Assessed	Judged
Quantified	Reviewed			

12. Where is your undivided attention?

Addressed	Investigated	Perceived	Studied	Examined
Inspected	Questioned	Surveyed	Measured	Read
Tested	Explored	Observed	Researched	Weighed
Experimented				

13. Are you a decision maker?

Activated	Approved	Decided	Resolved	Adopted
Concluded	Determined	Settled		

14. Got negotiation skills?

Arbitrated	Mediated	Reasoned	Settled	Balanced
Moderated	Reconciled	Solved	Intervened	Negotiated

15. What have you organized before?

Arranged   Complied   Coordinated   Prepared   Assembled
Compiled   Correlated   Structured   Categorized   Connected
Implemented   Summarized   Collected   Consolidated   Organized
Systematized   Combined

16. What do you operate?

Conducted   Handled   Performed   Repaired   Controlled
Implemented   Troubleshot   Tended   Fixed   Maintained
Ran   Used   Functioned   Operated   Rebuilt
Worked

17. What things do you document?

Certified   Logged   Recorded   Supported   Charted
Mapped   Researched   Tabulated   Documented   Proved
Substantiated

18. What do you frequently explain?

Defined   Detailed   Elucidated   Explained

19. What connections did you make?

Aligned   Connected   Matched   Merged   Networked

20. What did you understand?

Attributed   Grasped   Perceived   Translated   Discerned

Interpreted   Transcribed

21. How are you responsible?

Assured	Ensured	Protected	Secured	Confirmed
Guaranteed	Satisfied	Inspected	Delivered	Guarded
Safeguarded				

22. Exactly how are you future-oriented?

Estimated	Deterred	Predicted	Projected	Forecasted
Hypothesized	Prevented	Strategized		

23. When do you work with people?

Advised	Guided	Mentored	Reinforced	Coached
Influenced	Motivated	Rehabilitated	Convinced	Informed
Persuaded	Served	Counseled	Inspired	Prescribed
Taught	Educated	Instructed	Probed	Trained
Facilitated	Listened	Tutored	Recommended	

24. When were you part of a Team?

Advised	Conferred	Fostered	Participated	Aided
Consulted	Helped	Served	Assisted	Cooperated
Joined	Teamed-with	Collaborated	Facilitated	

25. When did you lead anything?

Acted	Governed	Led	Performed	Administered
Handled	Maintained	Piloted	Advised	Fostered
Managed	Processed	Conducted	Implemented	Motivated
Scheduled	Controlled	Inspired	Navigated	Showed

Directed   Influenced   Ordered   Supervised   Facilitated

26. How do you supervise employees?

Appointed   Employed   Hired   Referred   Awarded
Enforced   Interviewed Selected   Enlisted   Evaluated
Nominated   Staffed   Elected   Fired   Recruited
Terminated

27. When did you communicate something?

Communicated   Lectured   Related   Spoke
Demonstrated   Modeled   Reported   Submitted
Displayed   Persuaded   Represented Symbolized
Dramatized   Presented   Shared   Verbalized
Explained   Proposed   Showed   Wrote
Illustrated   Publicized

28. How do you describe your personality?

Agile   Confident   Intelligent   Risk-taking   Accommodating
Dynamic Intuitive   Motivated   Accountable   Effective
Leading Edge   Analytical   Articulate   Energetic
Organized   Authentic   Enthusiastic   Service-Oriented
Sincere   Experienced   Perceptive   Skilled
Flexible Powerful   Catalytic   Autonomous   Straight-forward
Growth-oriented   Producing   Supportive   Hardworking
Professional   Talented   Thinker   Humorous
Quick-study   Thorough   Versatile   Compassionate
Results-Oriented   Insightful

NOTE: Original 'action word' source was derived from:
FYI: Florida International University
(Business School)

ROCKSTAR JOB TOOLS

Relationships, Jobs, and Resumes:
LinkedIn.com
Monster.com
CareerBuilder.com
GlassDoor.com
TheLadders.com

Women's Closet:
PuttingMeTogether.com
CurvyGirlChic.com
DressForSuccess.org
BeautyBroadcast.net
GirlWithCurves.com

Get *job* help today @
Your Local Public Library

Men's Clothes:
RealMenrealStyle.com
AskAndyAboutClothes.com
KgStores.com
RibbedTee.com

Nontraditional:
WetFeet.com
Vault.com
ReferenceUsa.com (free access at your library)
UnitedWay.org

My Notes

My Notes

My Notes

My Notes

ACKNOWLEDGEMENTS

William Frank Porter

Cali Porter
London Porter
Julia Porter
Nicole McMiller
Randall Ferguson

Jon Alexander Martin
Danielle Milam
Sloane McHenry-LaMartina
Dominic French
Bryan Williams

Jerry Carter
Bubba Thornton
Mario Aguilar
Jim Murren
Ross Bryant

Nubia Cervantes
Cynthia Rodriguez
Bryan Lebo
Steve Forst
Alma Clark
Les Brown

James Malinchak
Jud Wilhite
Ted Cooper
Yvonne Suarez
Chris Bundren
Amanda Smith-Gates

Ken Mowad
Melissa Peters
Joe Stoner
Glenda Billingsley
Reginal Harris
Bruce Lee (memory of)

Alice Whetts (memory of)
Trevez McMiller
Jessica Tomlinson
Helen Porter-Ferguson
Troy Price

The Porter Family
Jim Rhodes
Steve Wynn
Ray Dinardi
Papy Saygbay

Monte Stratton
Melissa Peters
Thomas McCoy
Jennifer Reyna
Joe Micatrotto

Carla Land
Jared Lebo
Jo Anna Lebo
Scott Pelley
Felton Thomas
Milton Friedman (in memory)

Brendon Burchard
Joel Osteen
Courtney Lancaster
Tiffany Reardon
Joan Dunn
Regina Calhoun

Jonathan Sprinkles
Christine Bundren
Punam Mathur
Gunnar Kim
Rick Ross
John Legend

ABOUT THE AUTHOR

London refused to allow me to gloat on him; instead, he asked that I speak towards the service he provides his circle of influence, both locally and abroad. And that I use less than 250 words.

London's Core Energy Generation Factors are:
Photography, Writing, and Motivational Speaking/Exercise

He's an advocate for Youth and Military Service Members. London uses education as a foundation to service both missions.

The book **Rockstar Your Job Interview** and Video Series is NO COST to all Military Service Members. London stresses,

"nothing is free, everything costs time... far greater than money"

The works of **Rockstar Your Job Interview** is recognized in Australia, Canada, England, and Ireland. It's currently being translated into Spanish for South American distribution in 7 countries.

London lives in Las Vegas with his two children, Cali and London

Other Books by London:

Youth Motivation:
Who's Your Hoo: The Power of Mentorship
Business:
HR Rock Star: How to Get to The Boardroom and Stay There
Fiction:
Touch Rain

GO ONLINE @

www.ROCKSTARYOURINTERVIEW.com

To access *training videos* that accompany this book.

Made in the USA
Lexington, KY
07 March 2014